Copyright © 2016 by Lani Sharp
All rights reserved. This book or any portion thereof
may not be reproduced or used in any manner whatsoever
without the express written permission of the publisher
except for the use of brief quotations in a book review.

Printed in Australia

First Printing, 2015

ISBN 978-0-9945051-1-8

White Light Publishing House
6 Lincoln Way
Melton West, VIC, Australia 3337

www.whitelightpublishingau.com

❧ DEDICATIONS ☙

This book is dedicated to three very special Bulls: Carlie and Amber (a.k.a. 'Pigeon'), the two most inspiring Taurean girlfriends in my life's journey so far - both of you have given me such loyalty, warmth and understanding, and I am forever indebted to you both for your friendship.

Of course, the most honourable mention goes to my maternal Nana (born 5 May 1927), the second most enduring influence in my Universe after my mother. Nana, your lessons, love and deep wisdom impressed themselves upon my young mind and continue to guide me to this day. I loved and adored you; a part of my heart and soul went with you on the day you departed. You loved me unconditionally, like no one else has before or since. You are never forgotten.

ABOUT THE AUTHOR

☾ ★ ☽

Lani Sharp is a Natural Born Rebel who just also happens to be an Aquarian, who shunned 'conventional' astrology courses to pursue her own path in the wondrous, inspiring and ever-evolving field of cosmic forces and stellar influences. After failing to find a course or tutor that suited her needs, Lani set out on her own starry Magic Carpet adventure across the skies, partly to discover her own 'truths' about this ancient system, but mostly to prove that one can achieve absolutely anything, including and above all, their dream careers (or lifestyle), if they put their hearts and souls into it. A self-taught astrologer who takes the esoteric and spiritual approach to this much-loved popular art, she has been studying and effectively practising astrology since she was eight years old. When she is not writing about, channelling, practising or teaching astrology, she can be found living her dream life alternating somewhere between her home in Australia's stunning Tropical North or her second home in Victoria's beautiful Dandenong Ranges, enjoying tea parties with her highly imaginative Cancerian daughter, Allira, and their gnome and fairy friends, crystal-wishing, day-dreaming, believing in gnomes, pixies, angels, fairies, magic and miracles, honing her magickal * witchcraft skills, Moon-gazing, Sun-worshipping, Venus-channelling, Jupiter-drawing, assisting others to discover, unravel and follow their true spiritual paths ... or of course walking across rainbows!

* Not a mistake. Magick is a Wiccan variation of the word 'magic'.

★

ACKNOWLEDGEMENTS, CREDITS & GRATITUDE BLESSINGS

★

I would love to thank the following people and entities for their amazing contributions, interest, support and faith in me as I wrote the manuscripts for each of the twelve astrological Sun signs. Firstly, the biggest thank you goes to my Mum, Sandra, and my stepdad, Barry, for their unending support, love, advice, daily Skype conversations, acceptance of our geographical distance, and above all, their inner knowing that everything always comes together in the end. Your support of me and my dreams is appreciated beyond words. Secondly, gratitude to my wonderful partner, Travis, for his patience (no mean feat for a Gemini!), for supporting me every step of the way, and for his acceptance of my 'mad scientist' Aquarian mindset by never trying to break down the invisible 'laboratory' walls I built around myself while writing the books. I would also like to extend my enormous gratitude to the following: Allira, my little Cancerian 'crab' daughter, a soul in a billion, who also had to tolerate and operate within the bounds of her nutty professor mother's antics and focus throughout the writing of the books. Thank you to Nicola, my wonderful Facebook friend, for recommending White Light Publishing House, and of course to White Light Publishing House themselves, for pouring their faith and passion into my project from the very beginning - and an even bigger thank you to the wonderful people behind the company for publishing my work, Christie and Jess! Gratitude also goes out to my dear friends, both near and far, who have inspired in me so many ideas through simply being themselves - especially Amanda and Carlie. Amanda, you have always been my 'astrology buddy' and I have always enjoyed - and learned so much through - our discussions on all things astrology and star signs: the good, the bad and the ugly! Having someone like you off which to bounce thoughts and share ideas with, has always been immensely helpful and appreciated. I have saved my final thank you for The Universe, who always delivers to me exactly what I have asked for, without exception. The Universe is my ultimate *higher power*, my guiding light, my powerful driving force, my spiritual helper, my guardian angel, my eternal friend, my inner motivator, my sympathetic listener, my inspirational teacher, and the fulfiller of all my dreams, including this one, having my very first book(s) published, a long-held dream that stretches way back through the years to my days of being a mini dreamer, inquisitor and stargazer. The Universe has always believed in me, but perhaps more importantly, I have always believed in *IT*.

So to all of the above, I wish to say:

Thank you, thank you, thank you!

"We were born at a given moment, in a given place, and like vintage years of wine, we have the qualities of the year and of the season in which we are born"

Carl G. Jung

"There was a star danced,
and under that I was born"

William Shakespeare

INSPIRED BY ALL THE SIGNS

Aries imparted courage and boldness
And helped me dance away the pain
Taurus gave me hugs and comfort
And shelter from the rain
Gemini provided me with laughter
And taught me again how to have fun
Cancer nurtured and sustained me
By reflecting back my Sun
Leo reminded me there was joy
From within myself and above
Virgo awakened my healthy glow
By teaching me how to love
Libra gave me gentle hugs
And judged me not for a thing
Scorpio lent me some of his power
And took away the sting
Sagittarius showered me with gifts
Of words so wise and true
As Capricorn led the way up the mountain
My resolve and strength grew
Aquarius gave me the gift of friendship
And carried me as his brother
And Pisces swam with me to the depths
With a compassion like no other.

Special Note

Throughout the text of this book, and indeed the whole Lucky Astrology book series, I have capitalised the first letter of the word 'Universe'. This is because, quite simply, I feel it is a very special title for the higher power that I personally choose to be guided by, and have accordingly highlighted it as such.

You may also notice that I use the words 'he' or 'she', and 'his' or 'her', when referring to your own Sun sign and other zodiac signs, and never 'he or she' or 'his or her' together. The reason for this is for simplicity, for I don't wish the sentences to be too wordy and therefore the messages within them to be lost. As a general rule, I refer to all six 'masculine' zodiac signs as 'he', and all six 'feminine' signs as 'she', and this remains a consistent rule throughout this book and the whole series.

Your Sun sign, Taurus, is a feminine sign and will thus be referred to accordingly.

CONTENTS

	Page
ASTROLOGY	15
THE ZODIAC & YOUR PLACE IN THE SUN	24
TAURUS THE BULL	31
QUOTES BY TAUREANS	37
THE TAURUS CONSTELLATION	42
THE TAURUS SYMBOL	45
THE RUNDOWN & LESSONS ★	
THE ESSENCE OF TAURUS	48
THE THREE DECANS OF TAURUS	59
YOUR ELEMENT ★ EARTH	65
YOUR MODE ★ FIXED	85
YOUR RULING PLANET ★ VENUS	88
YOUR HOUSE IN THE HOROSCOPE ★	
THE SECOND HOUSE	101
YOUR OPPOSITE SIGN ★ SCORPIO	105
MAGIC, DRAWING, ATTRACTION, SPELLS,	
RITUALS, WISHING & POWER	113
ASTROLOGY & MAGIC	118
PLANETS ★ DAYS OF THE WEEK	
& THEIR POWERS	124
YOUR NATAL MOON PHASE	128
SPELLS, MAGIC & WISHING WITH MOON PHASES	131
THE MOON ★ WHAT T REPRESENTS IN THE	
HUMAN PSYCHE & NATAL CHART	138
YOUR MOON SIGN	141
YOUR BODY & HEALTH	149
THE CELL SALTS ★ ASTROLOGICAL TONICS	155

	Page
EARTH SIGN TAURUS & THE MELANCHOLIC HUMOUR	158
MONEY ATTRIBUTES	161
COLOURS ★ YOUR LUCKY COLOURS	164
LUCKY CAREER TIPS	180
LUCKY PLACES	184
GEMS & CRYSTALS	186
TAUREAN POWER CRYSTALS	198
YOUR LUCKY NUMBERS	209
YOUR LUCKY MAGIC HOURS OR TIME UNITS	217
YOUR LUCKY DAY ★ FRIDAY	222
YOUR LUCKY CHARM / TALISMANS	226
YOUR LUCKY ANIMALS & BIRDS	229
YOUR METALS	241
PLANTS, HERBS, SPICES, TREES, SHRUBS, FLOWERS, SCENTS & INCENSE	245
YOUR FOODS	250
YOUR LUCKY WOOD & CELTIC TREE ★ SYCAMORE & WILLOW OR HAWTHORN	253
THE POWER OF LOVE	260
LUCKY IN LOVE? TAURUS COMPATIBILITY	272
YOUR TAROT CARDS	289
LUCKY 13 TIPS	307
HAVE YOU PACKED YOUR MAGICAL BAG FOR THE JOURNEY?	310
A FINAL WORD ★ TAPPING INTO THE MAGIC OF TAURUS	311

LUCKY ASTROLOGY

By Lani Sharp

TAURUS

*Tapping into the Powers of Your Sun Sign for Greater
Luck, Happiness, Health, Abundance & Love*

"That which is above is like to that which is below, and that which is below is like to that which is above, to accomplish the miracles of one thing ... the Father thereof is the Sun, the mother the Moon."

The Emerald Tablet, Hermes Trismegistus (circa 3000 BC)

★ ASTROLOGY ★

Astrology: "Divination through the correlation of earthly events with celestial patterns"
'Real Magic', I. Bonewits, 1971

A BRIEF HISTORY

Astrology can be defined as the calculation and meaningful interpretation of the positions and motions of the heavenly bodies, and their correlation with human experiences. Its central concept is based upon this interconnectedness or correspondence between the stars and ourselves.

The word astrology is derived from the Greek word astron, meaning 'star' and logos which means 'word'. Astrology, therefore, literally means language of the stars. It is based on the ancient law known as 'As Above, So Below', otherwise known as the Law of the Macrocosm and Microcosm. The Macrocosm is the Universe, symbolised by the sky, the starry dome that we can see from the Earth; the Microcosm is us - humans, and all other life on Earth. 'As Above, So Below' is a well-known and deeply impressing maxim of Hermetic origin, inscribed upon the famed Emerald Tablet among cryptic wording by enigmatic figure, Hermes Trismegistus, around 5,000 years ago. These four powerful words are adopted by astrologers and believers in magic to explain, in very succinct wording, the meaning behind the art and science of celestial influences upon our earthly affairs.

Astrology and many other magical and occult studies, propose that we are not separate from the Universe, we are part of it. The Sun, Moon and planets all follow exact patterns of movement and their motions can be measured precisely by astronomers. The basic idea of astrology is that all individual parts of the Universe, from plants to animals, cooperate with each other and work together in harmony.

Anyone can apply astrological knowledge in their daily lives, but it hasn't always been like that. At one time, astrology was reserved only for Kings and nations, and only the court astrologer/astronomer could cast and interpret horoscopes. Ancient astrology and astronomy used to be one and the same. To be an astrologer, you first had to be able to interpret the stars in some systematic way, and then track the movement of the Moon and the planets against the background of the constellations.

Astrology, the knowledge and language of the cosmos, goes back to the ancient kingdom of Babylonia and was adapted by the Mesopotamians, Greeks, Egyptians and Romans to incorporate their own deities (as indicated in mythology). It is upon a combination of Greek and Egyptian interpretations of astrology that our present knowledge is based.

In the ancient Mesopotamian world, as far back as 800 BC, people lived precariously beneath the open skies. The skies and the stars which filled them, were the real founders of astrology. Today we are aware that the Sun and Moon exert a profound influence upon our Earthly affairs, but for our primitive ancestors, the heavens, the stars and the planets must have been a matter of great and mysterious significance. Early humankind, its senses influenced by natural processes of ebbs, flows, growth, decay and cycles, tended naturally towards a physical explanation of the Universe. At first, the movements of the planets - and all celestial occurrences - were observed as omens affecting the Ruler and his nation; it was only in Egypt in the fifth century AD that the casting of horoscopes for individual people and the calculation of the planetary positions at the time of birth became widespread.

The first astrologers, the Chaldeans, mapped the stars and later passed this knowledge and wisdom on to the ancient Greeks, who, during the third century BC, developed astrology into a science with the use of mathematical aids and instruments to measure planetary movements. The Greeks were the first to cast individual horoscopes. And it was the Greeks who associated the four elements with the signs of the zodiac. The word "zodiac" can be translated from Greek to mean the "circle or path of the animals." The Greeks not only had names for the twelve Solar phases but had symbols for each, and many correspond with the ones we use today.

The Greeks passed on much of their knowledge to the Romans. During the second century BC, Roman astrologers were primarily forecasters who were consulted frequently by rulers of the church and state. By the early third century AD, astrology co-existed with early Christianity. This harmonious co-existence was possible because it was considered that celestial bodies could foretell events, but did not determine the future - indeed, the stars seen by the shepherds at the time of Christ's birth were only predictors of his arrival. After the fourth century AD, Christianity strengthened and the popularity of astrology declined as Christian reluctance to support 'pagan' or 'superstitious' beliefs became more prominent. The Middle Ages saw a revival in astrology, with courses being taught in universities and other educational establishments, and connections were made between the zodiac, alchemy, herbs and medicine. Astrology was once again able to exist alongside the Church, although many remained suspicious of astrologers.

Around the beginning of the fifteenth century, academics of the Renaissance movement examined the past for knowledge, and ancient philosophies, including astrology, flourished; this coincided with arts and science movements developing. The famous prophet and astrologer Nostradamus lived during this period. Leonardo da Vinci depicted aspects of astrology combined with geometry in his art. Writers and poets of the time, including Shakespeare, alluded to zodiacal influences in their work.

During this period, astrology had numerous practical applications. Agricultural calendars were introduced, indicating favourable planting times according to the phases of the Moon; health and illness were linked with movements of celestial bodies; and emotional states and mental health afflictions correlated with the planetary positions.

Eventually, new ways of thinking led to a split between astronomy and astrology, and by the seventeenth century, the realm of science had developed to such a degree that astrology was no longer taken seriously.

The study of the sky above us has been charted for more than 5,000 years. This fact is known because ancient 'horoscopes' imprinted on clay tablets have been unearthed, dating back almost 5,400 years ago. However, no one knows for certain just how, when and where astrology first began, although it is known that it flourished in ancient Chaldea, Mesopotamia, Babylon and Egypt.

Astrology is a science which has spanned many centuries and still remains extraordinarily popular, and its truths have the potential to speak to and *through* all of us. Long before today's interest in it, men of great vision such as Ptolemy, Hippocrates, Plato, Galileo, Jefferson, Franklin, Newton, Columbus and Jung respected its inherent truths, mythology and eternal knowledge. Furthermore, astrology predates many other 'sciences' - for out of it grew religion, medicine and astronomy, not the other way around.

The discipline of astrology is ultimately a study of the interlocking and interrelated forces of the twelve zodiacal forces, or constellations, that grace the heavens, as they pour their energies into the earthly kingdoms below. As these various energies circulate throughout the etheric realm of our Solar system, these zodiacal entities and archetypes imprint their vibrational frequencies and harmonic resonances upon our bodies, minds, souls and spirits.

ASTROLOGY & THE INDIVIDUAL

Since the earliest period of the history of humankind, people studied the starry vaults of the heavens and conceived that their presence, movements and positions endowed planet Earth's inhabitants with Divine influence. There is much evidence that positions and movements of the planets as seen from Earth at the time of a birth are linked to personality characteristics of individuals. Human energy and emotional cycles are governed by the forces and networks of magnetic impulses from all the planets. Of all the heavenly bodies, the Moon's effects and power are the most marked and visible due to its close proximity to Earth. But the Sun, Venus, Mars, Mercury, Jupiter, Saturn, Uranus, Neptune and Pluto exercise their influences just as surely. In fact, scientists are aware that plants and animals are affected by natural cycles which are governed by forces such as fluctuations in barometric pressure, the gravitational field and electricity in the air. These Earthly dynamics are originally triggered by magnetic vibrations from the atmosphere, or outer space, from where the planets send forth their unseen waves. No living organism or mineral on Earth escapes these immense, if unseen, influences.

The geomagnetic field seems to affect life on Earth in certain observed ways, and these influences appear to correlate with planetary positions. It has been suggested that the fluctuations of the Earth's magnetic field are picked up by the nervous system of the in utero infant, which acts like an antenna, and these synchronise the internal biological clocks of the foetus which control the moment of birth. The foetal magnetic antenna therefore, is sensitive enough to sense these planetary vibrations and fields, and through a combination of inherited genetics and the positions of the planets at birth, they are imprinted with certain basic inherited and 'absorbed' personality characteristics.

Carl Jung, the Swiss psychiatrist and psychological theorist, suggested that the inherent disposition of the individual is present at birth, and is reflected in the patterns of his or her natal chart. Further, he theorised that there is a 'priori factor' in all human activities, namely the inborn, preconscious and unconscious individual structure of the psyche. The preconscious psyche, for example that of a newborn baby, is not simply an empty vessel into which practically anything can be poured, but rather it is this preconscious psyche that gives us the free will to become what we are instead of what others or our environment makes us. The child is not merely a receptacle for the psychic life of those around him or her, albeit sensitive and susceptible to the surrounding unconscious forces in childhood; for he/she also brings something of his own to his experience of them.

Further, Dr Harold S. Burr, who was a Professor of Anatomy at the Yale University School of Medicine, and author of *The Nature of Man and the Meaning of Existence* (1962), asserted that there is order in the Universe, unity in the organism and man is endowed with a soul. He stated that a complex magnetic field not only establishes the pattern of the human brain at birth, but continues to regulate and control it through life, and that the human central nervous system is a superb receptor of electro-magnetic energies, indeed the finest in nature. He contended that the electro-dynamic fields of all living things, which may be measured and mapped with standard voltmeters, mould and control each organism's development, health and mood, and named these fields 'fields of life'.

It can therefore be suggested that astrological and planetary influences endow us with the majority of our characteristics at birth, characteristics bestowed upon us according to our Sun sign and other planetary forces. Other parts of the chart are also highly significant and need to be integrated for a 'whole' picture to form, however the Sun sign is an excellent starting point.

The ancients taught that astrology was one of the keys to the many enigmas that plague humans in their unceasing quest to determine what the meaning of life is, and what their role and place in the Universe is - and this quest still persists today. Astrology, which dates back over 5,000 years, is indeed one such key to unlocking the many secrets of the Universe - and ultimately, the individual self.

"KNOW THYSELF"

"Man, know thyself.
All wisdom centres on this."
Carl Jung

Before the temple of the Oracle at Delphi, the ancient Greeks imparted a special piece of advice that was carved onto one of the portals: "Know Thyself." These two powerful words are easy enough to understand, but much more difficult to apply. Throughout life's inner and outer journey, astrology can provide us with an inner navigational system by which we can be guided towards our highest potential, and closer towards the eternal quest of 'knowing thyself'. It provides the hope that this higher spiritual plane exists and that if we can 'read' and therefore be guided by the unique inner blueprint that our individual birth chart has stamped upon us at the moment we take our very first breath, indeed we can reach this higher spiritual plane and realise our innate potential.

Always remember that astrology is not fatalistic. The stars may incline, but they do not compel. Astrology simply provides us with an inner guide, a blueprint, for our journey through life and the finding of our true selves - and what we do with the resulting knowledge is entirely up to us.

Good luck on your journey!

THE ZODIAC & YOUR PLACE IN THE SUN

The zodiac is a circle of 360 degrees, consisting of equal segments of 30 degrees each. These represent the twelve houses of the twelve astrological signs. This zodiac is how the early astrologers imagined the Solar system to be, a perfect circle with the Earth at its centre, around which the Sun, Moon and the planets revolved. Each sign of the zodiac corresponds to one of the twelve segments, following a chronological order and established according to the rhythm of the seasons and cycles of the Sun and the Moon. But the zodiac itself, or the band of constellations which comprise it, has shifted over the millennia, creating division between astronomical and astrological schools of thought. It has been said that due to this shift over time, one who once considered themselves as an Aquarian, is actually a Capricorn, the sign before it, and a Leo is actually a Cancerian, its preceding sign. This is the result of misunderstandings and differences in perspectives, and explanations around it are beyond the scope of this book, but can be researched further should you wish to delve a little deeper.

From the astronomical point of view, it is true that the zodiac to which we refer today is not situated where it 'should' be, but indeed, nothing is fixed under the celestial vault. And so the starting point of the ancient zodiac does not correspond exactly to the one we can observe today. But for the purposes of increasing your power and luck, let's keep things simple and enjoy the ride; after all, astrology - while based upon many scientific theories, mysteries, scepticism, superstitions, facts, measurable patterns, ambiguities, correlations, paradoxes, contradictions, links, stigmatisms and observations that seek to support, refute, prove and disprove this ancient art time and again - is ultimately meant to be *fun* too!

THE SUN

Earth's Luminary ★ *Our Brightest Shining Star*

Our Centre, Core Self, Identity & Inner Guiding Light

"Perfect is what I have said of the work of the Sun."
Hermes Trismegistus, The Emerald Tablet

The Sun is our essence, centre, source, ego strength, power, life force, will, vitality, creative expression, purpose, life's direction, our sense of identity, and who we really *are*. Our brightest star is the core of our individuality, our inner guiding light. The Sun is externalising, and represents totality, infinity, eternity, the striving toward and ultimate reaching of one's personal destiny, and *completion* in all areas. It is the creative energising giver of life and the 'father' of the zodiac. It endows us with our inherent creative potential and personal identity - our urge to *create* and to *be*. The Sun is our core self, conscious purpose, our sense of creating something out of our own being. It is the integrated personality and represents the *present*, our greatest Gift. The Sun rules the heart and is thus symbolically the centre of Self. Indeed, the Sun *is* the heart and the most commanding presence in our birth chart; the luminary Ruler who governs our essential self and wants to be noticed and appreciated, and above all, to *shine*.

★ KEY WORDS ★

Identity, core self, spirit, life force, power, essence, creativity, higher self, the Father, ego, vitality, pride, individuality, leadership, majesty, inner authority, will, expression, willpower, purpose, the journey, the path and the destiny.

THE SUN ★ THE ULTIMATE SOURCE OF LIFE ON EARTH

Throughout the ages, and indeed since life forms began, the electromagnetic waves generated by the Sun have kept planet Earth habitable for humans, animals, plants and minerals. The Sun is, in fact, the only true source of energy on planet Earth. It provides the perfect amount of energy for plants to synthesise all of the products required for growth and reproduction, which is then stored by plants and ingested by humans and animals who, through many complex processes, utilise these various forms of encapsulated Solar energy - and so the cycle continues. Wood, fuel and minerals (crystals included), too, are merely various forms of this encased Sun energy. In fact, all matter is essentially 'frozen' light. Human body cells are bundles of Sun energy; we couldn't conceive or process a single thought without the molecules of Solar-energised oxygen and glucose.

In essence, the Sun supports the growth of all species, including human beings and microscopic life forms, and without it life on Earth would simply not be possible. The mathematical and metaphysical complexity that stands behind a system of organisation and order so infinitely diverse and intricate as planetary life cannot be truly fathomed, but unerringly and miraculously, the Sun instinctively knows what each species, from a tree to a human, intrinsically needs in order to fulfil its evolutionary purpose and cycles.

Ultimately, the electromagnetic waves generated by the Sun come in a variety of lengths, which determine their specific course of action and responsibility. There are gamma rays, x-rays, cosmic rays, various kinds of ultraviolet rays, infrared, short-wave infrared, radio waves, electric waves, and of course the visible light spectrum, consisting of the seven colour rays.

Most of these energy waves are absorbed and used for various processes in the layers of atmosphere that encircle the Earth, and only a small portion of them - the electromagnetic spectrum - reach the surface of our planet. Although the human eye is only able to perceive about one percent of this spectrum, the waves exert a very strong influence upon us. The waves and rays which do affect us so profoundly, allow all life forms to undergo constant cycles of change necessary for growth and renewal. Physically, we can observe this, but on a deeper, more spiritual plane, we can even *feel* it and allow its radiance to permeate our very souls. Such is the might, force and power of that astonishing ball of fire in our sky: the brilliant, ever-shining Sun.

THE SUN ★ WHAT IT REPRESENTS IN THE HUMAN PSYCHE & NATAL CHART

☼

"The Sun is the most powerful of all the stellar bodies. It colours the personality so strongly that an amazingly accurate picture can be given of the individual who was born when it was exercising its power through the known and predicable influences of a certain astrological sign; these electromagnetic vibrations will continue to stamp that person with the characteristics of their Sun sign as they go through life."
Linda Goodman's Sun Signs, Linda Goodman, Pan Books, 1968

The Sun is our essence, our core self, conscious purpose and sense of identity, our creative potential, our spirit, the integrated personality that shines outward from within us. It is concerned with the present. It is our centre, source, power, life force, will, vitality, purpose, life's direction, what and who we *really* are.

The Sun represents our basic urge for self-expression. It is the 'Solar energy cell' in a person's character, the Lord and giver of life, and symbolises the way in which an individual will shine out to the world. Our Sun is our personal identity and aspects to it from other components in the chart show the ease or otherwise of assuredness and confidence with which one will project and express one's individuality. The Sun sign will also show how an individual bounces back from setbacks and disappointments, their resilience and their general outward expression of energy.

The Sun is the archetype of the Father and represents the primary masculine principle in the natal chart. It indicates how we express and experience our masculine side, or animus, our conscious self, how we express ourselves creatively, our personal potential, individuality, self-expression and personal power. It has to do with courage, power, generosity, creativity, vitality, self-confidence, nobility, self-worth, dignity and strength of will. It symbolises authority and purpose, the *ruler*, and its potential is the peak of constructive maturity. It signifies self-sufficiency and abundance, containing enough energy to radiate warmth and give life to everything around it.

The sign in which one's Sun is posited, and its placement in the birth chart, strongly indicates the level and type of vitality available to the personality (the sign), and in which area of life this may be most strongly directed (the house).

The Sun in a natal chart is a powerful symbol because everything is filtered, at a conscious level, through it. It tells us what we need to do to feel fully alive, the type of engine 'driving' us, what we need to do to be authentic and to be fully functioning. Listening to the special message of one's Sun sign can provide one with greater direction, and a more dynamic energy and life purpose.

The symbol for the Sun ☉ depicts a circle with a dot or 'seed' at its centre, from which the core self, power, creativity and the first sparks of life can spring. The circle around this 'seed' represents spirit, symbolising wholeness, eternity and the never-ending flow of energy.

While the Moon, the night sky's luminary, represents the *soul*, the Sun, the day sky's luminary, represents our *spirit*.

There is a reason your Sun sign is otherwise known as your Star Sign - it's because, quite simply, the Sun *is* a star; in fact, it's the largest, brightest, shiniest one in Earth's known visible Universe. This book is about your Sun sign and how you can become much larger, glow with far more brilliance, and shine brighter than you ever dreamed possible. I wish you all the magic in the galaxy for your dreams to come true and your deepest wishes to become reality, through tapping into the amazing power and inherent potential of your Sun sign. So get set for a galactical ride through the lucky stars of your constellation - and may a shooting star cross the path in front of you as you go!

TAURUS THE BULL

★ Fixed Earth, Negative, Feminine, Sensate ★

"My nourishment grows naturally from the Earth"

Body & Health
Throat, Tonsils, Neck, Thyroid, Thymus, Vocal Cords

How Taurus Emanates its Life Force / Energy
Steadily, thoroughly, productively, patiently

Is concerned with
★ Beauty, romance, sentimentality, sensuality ★
★ Materialism, prosperity, wealth ★ Comfort ★
★ Nature ★ Harmony ★ Dependability ★
★ Possession, control ★ Security ★
★ Habit ★ Tenacity ★ Kindness ★ Calmness ★
★ Peace ★ Gentleness ★ Affection ★

Spiritual Taurus

Your Archetypal Universal Qualities
The Earth Spirit, Manifester, Builder

What You Refuse
To change or give in

What You Are an Authority On
Resourcefulness, endurance, loyalty

The Main Senses Through Which You Experience Reality
Touch, substance, ownership, worth

How You Love
Sensually, warmly, enduringly

Positive Characteristics
★ Dependable ★ Offers enduring loyalty ★
★ Careful and conservative in outlook ★
★ Calm and patient ★ Trustworthy ★
★ Altruistic, attentive ★ Thorough ★
★ Resourceful ★ Solid ★
★ Loving and affectionate ★
★ Values the talents of others ★
★ Gentle, placid and consistent ★

Negative Characteristics
★ Self-indulgent and greedy ★
★ Stubborn, obstinate and can get stuck in a rut ★
★ Lazy, slow-moving and acting ★
★ Little to say ★ Dull ★
★ Controlling and possessive ★
★ Procrastinates by lengthy pondering ★
★ Insensitivity ★

To Bring Out Your Best

Cuddles, give and receive massages, clear out your clutter, do some gardening, have a luxury weekend away, consume good quality food and wine.

Spiritual Goals

To learn the value of insight; to delve deeper; to overcome obstinacy and truly see others' points of view on things; to steer clear of ruts; to focus more on spiritual wealth.

TAURUS

20 April - 20 May

Fixed Earth

Ruled by Venus

"I POSSESS"

Gemstones ◊ Emerald, Sapphire, Diamond

★ Patient, possessive, reliable, obstinate, warm-hearted, security-loving, determined, sensual, affectionate, passive, self-indulgent, unemotional, inflexible, loving, steady, stolid, persistent, consistent, materialistic, placid, nature-loving, arduous, industrious, gluttonous, unmoving, lazy, stubborn, complacent, domestic, laidback, dependable, rooted, conservative, enduring, composed, productive, trustworthy, constructive, strong, physical, calm, easy-going, slow, careful ★

"Nothing is impossible.
The word itself says 'I'm Possible'!"
Audrey Hepburn

TAURUS

♈

★ **Gentle** ★ **Sensual** ★ **Practical** ★
★ **Affectionate** ★ **Loyal** ★ **Warm** ★
★ **Patient** ★ **Reliable**

Taurus is the sign of the Bull, a steady, placid animal who is hard to move but once angered can dig those heels into the dust and charge with great, determined force. Stubborn, easy going, simple, sensual, indulgent, materialistic, obstinate, possessive, productive, patient, loyal and affectionate are Taurus' most notable traits. Being a solid Earth sign, this sign is practical, persistent and pragmatic, but can lack imagination, passion and spontaneity. Warm-hearted and loving, Taurus loves to give and receive affection and is romantic and consistent in its approach to love.

The Bull is materialistic and loves to be surrounded by beauty and the simple pleasures in life, such as good food, quality wine and of course Earthy and non-pretentious décor. Loyalty is a big thing for the sure and steady Bull's spirit, and he is said to be the most loyal of the zodiac, sometimes to a fault, such is their stubbornness and endurance in friendship and romance. Taurus is cautious and takes slow steps towards its goals, being ever careful to lay a solid foundation before it slowly builds upwards. A warm and affectionate lover, dependable friend and an industrious worker, Taurus is the second sign and the reliable strong 'rock' of the zodiac, never letting its emotions get in the way, possessing amazing common sense - the Bull never loses its head when all around are losing theirs, making Taurus reassuring and comforting to have around in the midst of life's chaos.

KEY CONCEPTS
★ Devoted, staunch loyalty ★
★ Unmoved and immovable ★
★ Slow, cautious and deliberate ★
★ Stubborn without just reason ★
★ Dry, staid and hard ★
★ Rational, level-headed and realistic ★
★ Overindulges sensual appetites ★
★ Greedy, pleasure-seeking and hedonistic ★
★ Materialistic and rigid ★
★ Steadfast, composed and calm ★
★ Grounded, rooted and stable ★
★ Affectionate and generous of heart ★
★ Firm, productive and fertile ★
★ Intensely sensitive and understanding ★

SOME CORRESPONDENCES THAT ARE ASSOCIATED WITH TAURUS

Good food, copper, fertility, Venus, love, luxury, jewellery, music, dependability, the throat, Earthiness, gardening, caution, fixed opinions, affection, financiers, horticulture, money, endurance, crops, stability, security, reliability, romance, stubbornness, stodginess, possessiveness, landscaping, musicians, treasurers, possession and ownership, slowness, charm, banks, artists, confectionary, beauty, art and bronze. Take your pick and enjoy the ride!

QUOTES BY TAUREANS

"If you are not doing what you love, you are wasting your time" - Billy Joel (9 May 1949)

"I have no desire to prove anything by dancing. I have never used it as an outlet or a means of expressing myself. I just dance. I just put my feet in the air and move them around" - Fred Astaire (10 May 1899)

"Think about what people are doing on Facebook today. They're keeping up with their friends and family, but they're also building an image and identity for themselves, which in a sense is their brand" - Mark Zukerberg (14 May 1984)

"The question is, are we happy to suppose that our grandchildren may never be able to see an elephant except in a picture book?" - Sir David Attenborough (8 May 1926)

"By giving people the power to share, we're making the world more transparent" - Mark Zukerberg

"There is no such thing as fun for the whole family" - Jerry Seinfeld (29 April 1954)

"People are not going to care about animal conservation unless they think that animals are worthwhile" - Sir David Attenborough

"Just don't give up on trying to do what you really want to do. Where there are dreams, love and inspiration; you can't go wrong" - Ella Fitzgerald (25 April 1917)

"One cannot accomplish anything without fanaticism" - Eva Peron (7 May 1919)

"A two-year-old is kind of like having a blender, but you don't have a top for it" - Jerry Seinfeld

"If there hadn't been women we'd still be squatting in a cave eating raw meat, because we made civilisation in order to impress our girlfriends" - Orson Welles (6 May 1915)

"Women are not in love with me but with the picture of me on the screen. I am merely the canvas on which women paint their dreams" - Rudolph Valentino (6 May 1895)

"If you can't stand the heat, get out of the kitchen" - Harry S. Truman (8 May 1884)

"Say yes, and figure the rest out afterwards" - Tina Fey (18 May 1970)

"When you have a dream you've got to grab it and never let go" - Carol Burnett (26 April 1933)

"A good artist should be isolated. If he isn't isolated, something is wrong" - Orson Welles

"When I was 14 I was the oldest I ever was. I've been getting younger ever since" - Shirley Temple (23 April 1928)

"People who read the tabloids deserve to be lied to" - Jerry Seinfeld

"It's easy to fool the eye but it's hard to fool the heart" - Al Pacino (25 April 1940)

"Religion is the sigh of the oppressed creature, the heart of a heartless world, and the soul of soulless conditions. It is the opium of the people" - Carl Marx (5 May 1818)

"If men are honest, everything they do and everywhere they go is for a chance to see women" - Jack Nicholson (22 April 1937)

"Dwelling on the negative simply contributes to its power" - Shirley McClaine (24 April 1934)

"A girl can wait for the right man to come along, but in the meantime that still doesn't mean she can't have a wonderful time with all the wrong ones" - Cher (20 May 1946)

"Social progress can be measured by the social position of the female sex" - Carl Marx

"I have to be alone very often. I'd be quite happy if I spent from Saturday night to Monday morning alone in my apartment. That's how I refuel" - Audrey Hepburn (4 May 1929)

"I don't need a man, but I am happier with one" - Cher

"There is nothing either good or bad, but thinking makes it so" - William Shakespeare (26 April 1564)

"I've always been bossy" - Shirley Temple

"Early on, if I was alone two or three nights in a row, I'd start writing poems about suicide" - Jack Nicholson

"Keep away from people who try to belittle your ambitions. Small people always do that, but the really great make you feel that you too can become great" - Mark Twain (21 April 1910)

"Paris is *always* a good idea" - Audrey Hepburn

"Summer's lease hath all too short a date" - William Shakespeare

"When I am an old woman I shall wear purple, with a red hat which doesn't go, and doesn't suit me. And I shall spend my pension on brandy and summer gloves and satin sandals, and say we've no money for butter." - Jenny Joseph (7 May 1932)

"If you can't stand the heat, get out of the kitchen." - Harry S. Truman (8 May 1884)

"Live! Yes! Life is a banquet and most suckers are starving to death." - Patrick Dennis, 'Auntie Mame' (18 May 1921)

"Strong reasons make strong actions" - William Shakespeare

"It's useless to hold a person to anything he says while he's in love, drunk, or running for office" - Shirley McClaine

"There is only one success - to be able to live your life in your own way." - Christopher Darlington Morley (5 May 1890)

"I believe in pink. I believe that laughing is the best calorie burner. I believe in kissing … I believe in strong when everything seems to be going wrong. I believe that happy girls are the prettiest girls. I believe tomorrow is another day. And I believe in miracles" - Audrey Hepburn

"There are three ingredients in the good life: learning, earning and yearning." - Christopher Darlington Morley

"Don't be afraid to go out on a limb. It's where all the fruit is" - Shirley McClaine

"The buck stops here" - Harry S. Truman

THE TAURUS CONSTELLATION

The signs of the zodiac are the twelve symbolic features that ancient people imagined while observing the heavens. They saw shapes, patterns, faces, and natural and supernatural beings in the stars, from which they established, over centuries, a kind of celestial hierarchy and system based upon their observations. Groupings of stars became constellations, and twelve of these constellations make up the zodiac, a Greek word meaning 'circle of animals', that we know today.

Star constellations are not really self-contained groups but are particularly bright stars that give the appearance of being close together and form distinctive patterns. These are the patterns that over the ages have been identified as animals, deities or mythological figures and heroes. The stars are the living past. We receive their light long after it has left the star itself and so they are a good focus for escaping from the parameters of time. Their stellar influence is analogous with the aura, the bio/psychic energy field surrounding humans, animals, plants, crystals and even places. These individual energy systems interact with the energy waves emanated by other people, and even the cosmic rays emitted by planetary bodies, for psychic energies are not limited by time or distance.

The Taurus constellation is quite clearly marked, with a V-shape of stars for his face. It is a large and significant constellation, containing two spectacular star clusters. Although the starry Bull's head component only has his frontal segments, the constellation of Taurus is rich in stellar components: a group of hot, bright stars surrounded by an ethereal blue glow of light, can be found in this constellation. The Seven Sisters (the Pleides) and Hyades, seven mythological maiden daughters, lie within this constellation also. The Hyades form the V of the Bull's face, the most noticeable feature of this V being a large reddish star which is clearly visible to the naked eye and is often referred to as the "Eye of the Bull." (This reddish star is not actually a part of the Hyades, but in the same line of vision as that star cluster). The Bull's horns are long and extend quite far from its head; near the southern horn is the lovely Crab Nebula, a wondrous cloud of stardust and fragments that are remnants of a star which exploded hundreds of years ago.

WISHING UPON YOUR STAR

The practice of wishing upon a star is familiar to most of us, and is a mystical superstition that is ingrained in many of us from childhood. As a nighttime ritual, you can wish upon your own sign's constellation or that of the sign whose energies you wish to call forth; indeed, you can wish upon any constellation you feel an affinity with. If you can't see a particular constellation in your night sky, you can always meditate on it in your mind, or you can use the traditional technique of wishing upon the first star you see, while reciting the popular rhyme: *Star light, star bright, first star I see tonight, I wish I may, I wish I might, have the wish I make this night!* Any one of the three rituals will hold power for your own special wish. Good luck!

THE TAUREAN SYMBOL ♉

Astrology uses symbols or 'glyphs' to represent the planets and signs. The glyph is made up of shapes representing the energy and physical matter of which the Universe is composed, and how these shapes are used in each symbol provide hints as to the properties of the sign or planet it represents.

The ancient view was that there were five elements: Fire, Water, Air, Earth and Ether (or Spirit). Ether is invisible energy, while the four tangible elements are known as 'matter'. Ether, as pure energy, cannot be influenced by any of the physical/matter elements, although it surrounds them and indeed fuels them. The Greek philosopher and scientist Aristotle regarded this idea as a circle (Ether/Spirit) with a cross (matter) in the centre. This glyph is used in astrology as a symbol for Earth, and the cycle of life. All the symbols used in astrology represent the relationship between energy and the 'matter' elements.

The glyph of Taurus depicts the face and horns of the Bull, in essence the Bull's head. It clearly shows the circle of Ether with curved 'horns'. This symbol represents the unlimited potentiality (always signified by an empty circle) of the feminine principle in the Universe (shown by the crescent, here lying on its back and exalted over the circle to denote absolute receptivity and the predominance of instinct). The symbol of the Bull, an animal which can either be yoked to plough the earth or goaded into dangerous activity, represents the fertility of nature and the power of natural resources placed at the disposal of the spirit. 'Bully' is a word associated with the sign. The Bull has a powerfully developed neck, the part of the body ruled by this sign. This glyph contains the circle of spirit and the half-circle of soul; the Spirit seems to be supporting the Soul. This symbol is sensual and all-feeling, as there are no straight lines.

This symbol also illustrates the fecundity of Taurus, for it is representative of the fertile Full Moon with a crescent Moon attached, the Moon having celestial maternal associations and representing the principles of new growth and fertility. The semi-circle on top of the circle of Spirit may also symbolise Taurus being a receptacle for material wealth and abundance; the upturned 'cup' is open, awaiting gold in all its forms to be poured in and received.

THE AGE OF TAURUS ★ 4000 - 2000 BC

The Age of Taurus saw a growth in art and the emergence of the first population centres. This period of time was at the end of the Stone Age and it was during this period that the Egyptians began to smelt copper, the metal associated with Venus, Taurus's ruling planet. By this time, many countries were enjoying the benefits of agriculture, which led to a widespread growth in population centres as people abandoned their hunter/gatherer lifestyles for a more settled, rooted existence. Taurus is a Fixed Earth sign and this is reflected by the people of the Taurean Age who settled 'fixed' locations and cultivated the land (Earth). Once liberated from the demands of survival, people were freer to pursue and develop other talents such as art and architecture. The proliferation of artistic creations and works during this time, is perhaps attributable to this idea. It was also during the Age of Taurus that many cultures began to worship bulls, among them the Bull of Minos, and the Minotaur or the Cretan Labyrinth; and the holiness of cows - and of course Bulls - in the Hindu faith was born.

THE RUNDOWN & LESSONS
SOME QUIRKS, ODDITIES, UNIQUE CHARACTERISTICS & IDIOSYNCRASIES OF TAURUS

"The far-off Venus showers him with the love of luxury, he pays dearly for his possessions and treasures them for a lifetime. His home is his castle - and let no man disturb the peace of the Bull. Taurus is as patient as time itself, as deep as the forest, with a dependable strength that can move mountains."
Linda Goodman

There are two types of thinkers: what I like to call 'right-brainers' and 'left-brainers'. The left hemisphere of the human brain deals with things such as control of speech, verbal functions, logic, reason, mathematics, linear concepts, details, sequences, the intellect and analysis; the right hemisphere is concerned with spatial, music, holistic, artistic concepts, as well as simultaneity and intuition. You could go on to say that the left brain is masculine or yang in quality, and the right brain is feminine or yin in quality. Based upon these very simplistic outlines, it can be further stated that Earth sign Taurus dwells mainly in the right hemisphere, with a healthy dose of left thrown in for good measure.

What has been begun or initiated in Aries, Taurus begins building on. Seeking to give form to the impulse of life that the Ram has passed onto them, this sign gathers energy in material form, shows matter at its densest, and deals only with tangible reality. Generally dismissive of religion or abstract philosophies, unless it is concrete and real in a material sense, Taurus cannot grasp it or use it. It finds difficulty in changing direction and finds action meaningless without purpose and a firm direction.

Strong and silent characterises the typical Bull. If she's left alone and not disturbed, she will be utterly content. Taurus has straightforward and uncomplicated goals, and its energy creates repeating stable activity that brings results every time. Known for its productivity, possessiveness and pragmatism, Taurus relates most strongly to the material, manifest world. The Earth element and Fixed quality of Taurus makes it like an old, strong oak tree, well-rooted in the ground. Immovable and slow-growing, this sign operates at its own speed and in its own time. You innately recognise that it takes a long time for the seed to grow into the towering tree, and therefore you never rush into anything or try to hurry anyone, including yourself. Indeed, you need to make sure the roots are securely embedded before moving onto anything else. Negative, cool, dry, melancholic and stable, a determined (Fixed), practical and pragmatic (Earth) approach characterises the sign of Taurus.

Taurus was vitally important in the Egyptian seasonal calendar, most importantly for the fact that Taurus was once the beginning of the zodiac (and Aries, rather than Pisces the final sign). The star Aldebaran, in the middle of Taurus, was called 'The Bull's Eye', and was instrumental in fixing the starting point of the zodiacal circle, which indicates that the zodiac and perhaps astrology itself, underwent its formative period when the verbal equinox was in Taurus. Although an oversimplification, the Taurean Age was characterised as a matriarchal era in which the worship of the Bull was paramount. However, it wasn't the Bull per se that was the focus of the Age of Taurus, but rather growth, fertility, and the cycles of sprouting and abundance inherent in nature and in humankind, which are all associated with the sign of Taurus. Further, Taurus has long been strongly associated with the Moon just as much as with Venus, her planetary ruler. It is therefore perhaps no coincidence that the Moon is related to these cycles and it is also exalted in Taurus, meaning it expresses its energy harmoniously in this sign.

Taurus is the first of the Earthy signs and is ruled by the planet Venus. People born under this sign are generally enduring, patient, dependable, loyal and loving. Though you take a long time to build trust in another, once this is accomplished, you are ever present in your devotion and staying power. Taurus is the most yin of the zodiac signs and is sensual, affectionate, focused on establishing a stable and secure physical life rooted in the one place, but can be slow to respond, resistant to change, inclined to become stuck in a rut, and overly conservative.

With quiet, understated determination, Taurus plods patiently through life in a steadfast, deliberate manner. Stoic and emotionally robust, you take everything in your stride and not much frazzles, fazes or upsets you. You are as predictable as the Sun rising and setting, and this makes you the most dependable and trustworthy of all the signs.

You are the 'builder' of the zodiac, she who takes the fanciful ideas and schemes of your less-grounded zodiacal brothers and sisters, and makes them work, using the simplest of methods: sheer hard work and persistent effort. You of all people know there are no easy options, and 'soonest started, soonest finished' is your motto. You can be relied upon to put 110 per cent effort into everything you do, and you will rarely abandon a project halfway through. With great staying power, no matter how arduous the task, you will see it through to the end. This gives you great satisfaction, to see something begin at base level and be gradually built skyward. No matter how far into the clouds any project goes, however, you will remain firmly planted at ground level; shooting off into the stars does not appeal to your Earthy nature.

Essentially a homebody, if you don't own your own home yet you are probably dreaming about it, and you are likely to feel most comfortable and 'at home' in as natural surroundings as possible. Closeness to the Earth is important, if not vital, to your wellbeing and you usually strive to incorporate nature into your surroundings in any ways possible, even if just through having a flower and herb window box.

Determination is the key feature of the typical Taurean personality, and a reliable, cautious nature is also inherent. You are inflexible and adverse to risky behaviours, preferring the security and safety of a consistent routine and sameness of duties. You can display incredible stamina under pressure, and your stoicism and conformity is difficult to shake - this makes you an excellent person to have around in a crisis, for you will approach anything that needs to be done with calm patience and a diligent attitude.

Sometimes you may let that Earth fall away a little to reveal a more light-hearted side; expressing your love of music, the arts and the good life is evidence of this. Underneath your 'strong, silent type' cloak, you are a pleasure-seeker of the highest order and class and have a deeply sensual and self-indulgent personality.

You prefer to rely on information received through the five physical senses than any other-worldly realms, and you could never be accused of being irrational or illogical. Indeed, you consider everything thoroughly and thoughtfully before speaking or acting. Once a decision has been reached, you seldom reconsider, for you are the most fixed of the four Fixed signs and as such have firmly held opinions. Although you are not an overly emotional type, due to your need for security the feelings that most resonate with you are jealousy, obstinacy and possessiveness. You do not let go easily - this applies to both your material possessions and to relationships. If your sense of ownership or security is threatened, you will unleash a furious temper that lurks beneath your calm exterior. And you know what they say about red rags to Bulls! Resentment and simmering, repressed anger can also run deep in the Taurean's psyche. You can find it difficult to appreciate other points of view, and this is what leads to you forming entrenched opinions. You can go on for long periods of time exhibiting perfect poise and control, but if someone pushes too hard, puts too much pressure on, or piles the last straw on your sturdy back, you can unleash a rage like no other. Although you rarely get mad, you have the power to demolish everything in your path - like the proverbial Bull in a china shop, and all that subtlety and grace will fly out the window. Momentarily of course, because once the dust has settled, the peace, control, equilibrium and harmony that is so typical of Taurus will once again reign. Because you are normally so placid and it takes so much to provoke your rage, it is pretty much guaranteed that the perpetrator will not push the issue again. Your blind fury can be frightening to say the least.

Eminently practical in thought as well as deed, you call a spade a spade, not an 'agricultural digging implement'; analysis perplexes you, delving into depths irritates you. You are no-nonsense, saying what you mean and meaning what you say. More than any other sign, what you see is what you get with a Bull, for you grow impatient with dilly-dallying and more whimsical types who stop to smell every rose - and then write poetry about it! That's not to say you're not romantic or enjoy smelling roses yourself, you'd just prefer not to put too much thought into something that is a basic, indulgent pleasure. Complementing your practical side is a down-to-Earth brand of creativity and a deep, if latent, artistic ability.

Taurus adores luxury and all that is good and comfortable in life. Your artistic awareness is highly developed and you may also be musically talented. With your outstandingly strong sense of values, you believe in value and quality for money, and you're prepared to buy the best of everything. If you can't afford the best, you will save your pennies and go without until you can, for material security is important to you and possessions are vital to your wellbeing and your senses, particularly beautiful, luxurious ones. But you are never completely swept away by what you own, for you will always deal in tangibles, never pie-in-the-sky, however glamorous the packaging of person or product. But although it may seem like you have a 'no-frills' aura about you, you are in fact extremely sensuous, and have an enhanced sensitivity to beauty and a fine appreciation of what is pleasing to the senses. Physical satisfaction and romantic pleasures are important, if not vital, to you.

You tend to cultivate loved ones who are as straightforward, decent and honest as you are, and there is simply no friend stauncher or more loyal than your delightful self. When you commit yourself to a friendship, it's usually for life, through thick, thin, and all kinds of weather.

You are steady and calm, the most firmly planted sign of the zodiac, and indeed of the Earth signs. Your love of peace, home and family, and your caring, sensual nature endears you to others. The world of comfort, beauty, touch and the other physical senses motivates you, yet it can also entrap you. Taureans more than most have a way of getting stuck in a rut and bogged down in so many indulgences and material 'needs' that both health and hearth can suffer. Your Fixed mode also gives you an inflexibility that makes it difficult for you to change course or change your mind; you would rather stubbornly press on than to alter your path, especially if it is a comfortable and familiar one. Change and adaptability are not your strong points.

Sustaining is the principle with which Taurus is strongly connected. Astrology considers Taurus to be the most fertile, fruitful and constant sign. Despite her arguably frustrating tendency to be slow to act or be intolerably stubborn, Taurus, like the bull animal itself, steadies and roots herself in one place until she's ready to move. Then, as if a red flag were waved in her face, she becomes a formidably mobile force. She won't move until she's well and truly ready, though. And this is where the Taurean temperament is unique - she is unmoved and immovable, the epitome of pure, solid *Fixed Earth*.

Taurus is associated with fixity, fertility and fruitfulness, and as such she makes a wonderful gardener. Not every Bull is a green thumb, but most will definitely lead lives that closely parallel the cycles and concepts of nature. She is proficient at nurturing and sustaining all the metaphorical seeds she plants, and sees them through to full growth with unwavering patience and endurance. Due to her close inborn relationship with nature, when Taurus lives her life in accordance with the four seasons, she exists in harmony with her own nature. Because she is a Fixed sign and doesn't always flow easily with the tides of the changing seasons (or any changes for that matter), Taurus often gets bogged in life.

Your innate trust in your own natural instincts and abilities manifests as an expression of your Venusian sense of 'I have and I hold', an abundant loving energy which supports and strengthens everything and everyone it touches. Your instincts will also lead you to build a nurturing home environment, stability of income, and strong foundations in both character and your surroundings.

Loyalty and indulgent sensuality are the Bull's forte, an appealing combination which wins friends and lovers alike. You entertain loved ones lavishly and one would be hard pressed to find a more pleasant and accommodating host than a Taurus. Sometimes your lack of imagination or your possessiveness and stubbornness can prove stumbling blocks, but through learning to lighten up and experiment with new ideas and interests, your relationships will take on a new zest.

Astrologers are quick to characterise Taurus as plodding, slow-paced and materialistic, often forgetting to note your inherently artistic streak. Taureans are likely to be noteworthy in the arts, particularly in areas involving music and singing. William Shakespeare, a Taurus, richly described nature in his plays, and glorified the seasons and cycles, as well as expressing outrageous romance and abundance in his work.

As well as being talented in the arts, the archetype of the master craftsperson could be said to be quintessentially Taurean. You are a builder, and of all the signs, know how to first lay down the proper foundations for anything in life before you begin the often arduous task ahead. In this way, nothing deters you and your patience is unending. Taurus is the most likely sign of the person who, when given five hours to chop down a tree using a handsaw, will spend four and a half hours sharpening the saw first.

With your Sun in Taurus, you are naturally financially capable and possess the 'Midas touch', but need to beware that your assets and material goods don't consume you as Midas's did.

Your reputation for obstinacy comes from the combination of Earth and the Fixed nature of your sign, and this fixity applies to all your opinions and actions. Strongly resistant to change, you have an unyielding strength that will often keep you in the same spot out of fear, stubbornness and even a bit of Bullish pride, hence the Bull's well-known habit of becoming stuck in a rut. However, this can work for or against the powerful Bull. Dwelling in sameness lends you a charming and endearing consistency and simplicity of character that serves to support and sustain others - and of course yourself.

LESSONS TO BE LEARNED FOR GREATER POWER, ENLIGHTENMENT & LUCK

Taurean problems and ultimate undoing's arise through your archetypal grudge-bearing, smouldering anger, brooding silence, entrenched opinions, possessiveness, self-indulgence, jealousy, resentment, misplaced envy, lack of true depth, refusal to develop your character and inability to forgive or budge from a slight, whether perceived or real. An overwhelming attachment to money and material possessions and your tendency to seek security in external things, are also the Bull's weaknesses, and creates life challenges for your stubborn and slow-to-change nature.

Be wary of over-reliance on money and work on developing your spiritual side. Delving deeper into your spiritual self will help you overcome your natural tendency towards the urge of ownership of people and things. You need to learn how to forgive sincerely, realising that true emotional freedom can be found in surrendering to the hurts of the past and releasing any hard feelings you feel towards those who inflicted them. Let your gentle light shine through.

THE THREE DECANS OF TAURUS

Decans are thirty-six groups of stars that rise in a particular order on the horizon throughout each Earth rotation. These decans were developed in Egypt thousands of years ago. The rising of each decan marked the beginning of a new 'decanal hour' of the night for these ancient people, and eventually three decans were assigned to each zodiac sign. Each decan covers ten degrees of the zodiac wheel, and is ruled by different planetary rulers that rule over the other two signs of the same element (and a traditional ruler, when only seven of the planetary bodies were known). Decans continued to be used throughout the Ages, in astrology and in magic, but many modern astrologers, for whatever reasons, tend to disregard them. Following are brief descriptions for each decan of Taurus. Which one do you belong to? Can you relate to the description and the energies of your decan's ruling planet?

FIRST DECAN TAURUS ★ April 20 - 30

Ruler ★ Mercury (traditional *) / Venus (modern)

Keyword ★ Sensible

First Decan Taureans' Three Special Tarot Cards
The Hierophant, King of Pentacles & Five of Pentacles

Birthdays in this decan range from 20th April to 30th April. This is the Taurus decan, ruled by Mercury * and Venus. Taureans born during this decan possess a practical, dogmatic and determined character, and you will demonstrate an attachment to material things, but also oddly enough, thanks to Mercury's influence, to more ethereal concepts such as learning and the acquisition of knowledge. Common sense, practicality, fixed ideas, the need to feel secure and a determination to satisfy your desires, are all reinforced. Sensuous and pleasure-seeking, you may also blow hot and cold at times, thanks to a Mercurial temperament which makes you occasionally change direction, but this is usually a ploy adopted to manipulate others into getting things done for you so you can achieve your ultimate goal of comfort and material wealth. Stability is important to you and you seek out faithful, strong partners.

SECOND DECAN TAURUS ★ May 1 - 11

Ruler ★ Moon (traditional *) / Mercury (modern)

Keyword ★ Fertile

Second Decan Taureans' Three Special Tarot Cards ★ The Hierophant, King of Pentacles & Six of Pentacles

Birthdays in this decan range from 1st May to 11th May. This is the Virgo decan, ruled by the Moon * and Mercury. Taureans born during this decan possess a strong sense of discrimination and discernment, and can intuitively feel when things are not quite right and go about fixing them until they are just so. The Moon's influence puts an emphasis on your emotional and sensual values, and you place great importance on a fulfilling, satisfying love life. You will also have a strong attachment to and pull towards the natural environment, seeking out peace and quiet so you can steadily go about getting your life's work done. You have a robust ambitious streak, but it is cloaked in conservatism; you would prefer your work to be productive and fertile rather than loud and boisterous. Although you have an in-built sense of caution, you also leave leeway for negotiation and a knack for manoeuvring with skill and finesse. Charming, easy going and tactful, you are gifted with a natural flair for communicating ideas and thoughts to others. Overall you have a pleasant nature and a 'what-you-see-is-what-you-get' character, being generally open and honest.

THIRD DECAN TAURUS ★ May 12 - 20

Ruler ★ Saturn (traditional *) / Saturn (modern)

Keyword ★ Realistic

Third Decan Taureans' Three Special Tarot Cards ★ The Hierophant, Knight of Swords & Seven of Pentacles

Birthdays in this decan range from 12th May to 20th May. This is the Capricorn decan, ruled by Saturn *. Taureans born during this decan are characterised by a strong sense of duty, a respect for authority and a tendency towards traditional work and lifestyles. You are most comfortable when dwelling in a material and tangible reality, and are conservative and sensible. You are also ambitious, powerful, tenacious, determined and show a great commitment to feelings and convictions, albeit in a serious manner. Indeed, you take your responsibilities very seriously and always honour all your obligations and stick to a strict moral code. You do need to lighten up occasionally, as you can be prone to melancholia and self-criticism. And although you follow your path with an admirable single-minded devotion, you may also be inflexible and rigid to other people and closed off to new ideas. Loyal, disciplined and patient, you hold those you love dear and will go to any lengths for them. You also execute all your tasks to perfection, often resulting in great success and the material gain and security that you so seek.

The decan's traditional ruler based on the Chaldean order of the planets

YOUR ELEMENT ★ EARTH

According to the *Oxford English Dictionary*, the word *element* has a mysterious origin, and was first found in Greek texts meaning 'complex whole' or 'a single unit made up of many parts'. From the ancient up to medieval times, there were only four elements - Earth, Air, Fire and Water - and the occult-oriented also believed in a fifth: Spirit, or Ether. (Cornelius Agrippa called Spirit the 'quintessence'.

Alchemy is a tradition of visions and dreams, and images can combine on different levels of reality. Alchemists have long used images in their illustrations to express the enigma and mystery of their art, and to include all dimensions of our experience. The traditional worlds of Earth, Water, Fire and Air symbolise these dimensions very well. Broadly speaking, and in human terms, Earth corresponds to the level of the body and the senses, Water to the flow of thoughts and feelings, Fire to inspiration and energy, and Air to the world of the higher mind and intellect. Each of these worlds has its own realm of imagery. Taurus belongs to the realm of the Earth element.

★ The Practical Group ★

The path to SERVICE & DUTY

Focused on Materiality and Security

Alchemical Associations ★ The Physical, the Mineral Salt and the Colour Black

Key Attributes ★ Stability, Balance, Patience, Practicality, Realism

Governed by ★ The Physical Body and Sensations

Symbolism ★ Groundedness, stability, structure, protection, solidity, common sense, connection to the material and physical planes, and the five senses

Governed by ★ The Tangible and the Sensory

Earth Characteristics ★ Grounded, Practical, Balanced, Realistic, Materialistic, Solid

★ THE MAGIC OF EARTH ★

Earth is the solid rock on which everything else is grounded. It provides the soil for the roots you need to lay down at some point in your life, and yields the minerals and food you need to survive and thrive. Earth is the provider, the protector, the material aspect of the world and of yourself. If you have forgotten to keep both your feet on the ground, your dreams will carry you away - Earth is needed to provide grounding for them. Earth is supportive and reminds you that everything in life needs to be built on solid, sound, dependable foundations. The element of Earth is indeed life's great anchor.

★ KEYWORDS ★

Cautious, methodical, organised, predictable, substantial, stable, reliable, practical, pragmatic, sensual, patient, enduring, productive, grounded, persevering, dependable, useful, sensible *

"Earth is both of this world and the Otherworld, for she is host to all the other Elements besides: Air doth blow upon her face, Fire doth ignite within her belly and spew forth from her mountains, Water flows through her deep valleys, and Spirit marketh upon her skin the sacred pathways of our quest. Earth is our dwelling till we pass beyond into the secret glades of Otherworld, yet whilst we do live in human form then shall we honour and respect the Earth whence we came."

**Merlin's Book of Magick and Enchantment,
Nevill Drury**

Earth is the material substance principle. It gives form and substance to manifest what Fire has inspired and initiated. Earth is associated with the sensation function and its motivating force is material gain and security. Characterised by function, practicality and solidity, Earth seeks straightforward engagement with the physical world, mastery of it through efficient organisation and structure, and attainment of physical and economical comforts, respect, prestige and status. Taurus represents personal development, Virgo represents interpersonal development, and Capricorn represents transpersonal development. They are feminine polarity, introverted in expression.

In ancient legends, the Earth was regarded as maternal and protective, symbolising abundance and fertility. In mythology, Gaia or 'Mother Earth' was one of the first beings to emerge, along with Ouranos 'Father Sky'. They were bound by the ocean which whirled in an endless circle, keeping them together.

Earth is a complex and intriguing element, for when we think of it, we think of two things: the planet Earth, and the actual stuff our planet has as its base: soil, rock, and 'ground'. Earth connection is essential to having a grounded anchor for our magic to manifest; when Earth supports our 'work', we have a solid foundation for lift-off into the stars. Earth is like a home-base, a launching pad, and represents security, groundedness, foundations, practicality, the 'seen', tangible realities, and quite literally everything that has a has a down-to-Earth quality about it. Our desires begin and end with this element, and it is a great leveller; indeed, from it we all emerge and unto it we return.

Earth is the Universal archetype of the Divine feminine. Our planet is affectionately referred to as Mother Earth, the Great Mother, and Gaia, among many other names. Symbolising the inexhaustible spirit of creation, she is associated with abundance. When we work with this element, not only are we calling upon the powers of the mountains, caves, minerals and deserts that comprise its wondrous expanse, but we are also invoking its support and massive strength, for from it emerges abounding hidden treasures, giving us proof that material things can indeed be manifested from the Divine, deep and dark.

Throughout the history of magic, the element of Earth has been associated with a variety of deities, spirits and angels. And from the magical, as well as the esoteric and alchemical viewpoints, Earth has the lowest vibration of the four elements because it is so solidly manifest in our world. Rooted in practical concerns, it governs the primal facets of lie and of physical regeneration. It provides all we need for life, in the form of nourishment and shelter, and also provides material comforts and wealth. The treasures nurtured deep under its surface are testament to this, and have been long been yielded by mining methods and their ownership. Such treasures include gold, silver, other precious minerals, crystals, resources and other materials.

As the element suggests, Earth signs are down to Earth and self-sufficient. Pragmatic and conservative, they need structure and routine to feel safe and secure. Whether a practical Taurus, analytical Virgo or determined Capricorn, Earth signs approach life with caution and careful, methodical planning. Earth signs are not spontaneous by nature and do not like surprises or sudden changes, preferring a predictable and stable life. They tend to be organised, patient, calm, reliable, steadfast and provide a voice of reason, serving as a rock in loved ones' lives; they can indeed be truly relied upon in a crisis. However, their poised and modest nature sometimes makes it difficult for others to gauge how they are feeling or to prompt them to express their emotions.

Although Earth signs have sophisticated tastes and are strongly associated with materialism, they never manifest them in superficial ways, preferring to work hard, set goals and aim high. In essence, they strive to create a life free from money troubles and drama. They are tactile and sensual and though they may not be overly demonstrative (with the exception of Taurus), they are sentimental and affectionate in their own genuine ways.

In Earth we see the great cycles of nature and the effects it has on all the other elements. Though the cycle of the seasons relies upon the Sun, these seasons would become stagnant and motionless if it weren't for the movement of the Earth. For that reason, the mysteries of life, death and rebirth can be associated with this element - and although it is the Water element's inherent nature to explore these things on a deeper, more spiritual plane, Earth is the starting point for this exploration.

The Earth signs are sense-orientated, experiencing the world through a physical body. Concerned with security issues and moulding matter into form, Earth is productive, sensual and fertile. Earth supports, embodies, incarnates, contains, protects and provides a sense of groundedness. It is in the here and now, dealing with the present. Materialistic and sometimes power-hungry and greedy, the Earth element can also lack imagination and spontaneity.

The Earth element is firmly planted, coherent, has a sense of continuity, sustaining, follows things through, is sensory, sensual, resourceful, appreciative of beauty, pleasure-seeking, aesthetically aware, regular, containing, limiting, rigid, makes real, gives form and substance, is predictable, ritualistic, routine, enduring, reliable, committed, passive, conservative, stagnant, and sensitive to fertility and cyclical changes.

Although gravity pulls downward toward the Earth, mountains rise above it, and are associated with the Earth sign Capricorn. The first sign of this element, Taurus, represents the ground or soil, the second Virgo represents what is planted and grown in the soil, and Capricorn represents the high mountainous backdrop.

This energy is heavy, moving downward, symbolically anchoring us to our own personal ground. Earth signs are motivated by the desire to establish financial, physical and emotional security - through a steady job, money in the bank, a stable relationship.

Earth symbols include tortoises, caves, underground tunnels, mines, grottos, soil, rocks, minerals, farms, fields and mountains.

To start connecting with the 'Earth Spirit' realm, you can choose to concentrate on the spirits of the Earth - also known as devas - beginning with trees, flowers, soil, and of course Mother Earth herself. The Earth is an incredible, breathing, pulsating, living, vibrating spirit, majestically supporting all life on our planet. Also known as Gaia, she is the organic Mother of all of us, and becoming sensitive to her energy is to instantly feel physically stronger, securely supported and sustained.

Positive Earth Qualities ★ Earthy types are practical, hard-working, sensible, enduring, efficient, organised, realistic, patient, self-disciplined, conservative, persistent, common-sensical, unpretentious, stable, dependable, and capable of running households or businesses with a cool, pragmatic, unhurried, unfettered efficiency. Other positive traits of Earthy types are the following: Rooted, industrious, strong, determined, calm, goal-oriented, responsible, tenacious, sensual, committed, steady, concrete, cautious, grounded, solid, secure, robust, methodical, achieving, enduring, strong-willed, receptive, retentive, physical and reliable.

Negative Earth Qualities ★ Earthy temperaments can lack vision which may hold them back and they can become narrow, too 'rooted' in the one place, unadventurous, rigid, sluggish, resistant, immovable, and obstinate. They can also express their weaknesses in other not-so-desirable traits: Slow, stodgy, uninspired, unimaginative, petty, excessively conventional, dull, overly-cautious, narrow in perspective, stubborn, lacking in spontaneity, resistant to change, staid, hoarding, ultraconservative, inflexible, wilful, stingy, resistant to change, unoriginal, lethargic, closed-minded, over-reliant on the physical senses, overly conforming, lacking in perspective and spontaneity, selfish, bossy, heavy, bound by routine and rules, plodding, bureaucratic, perfectionism, possessive, dogmatic, controlling, authoritative, fussy, self-indulgent, fearful, suspicious, pessimistic, melancholic, critical, materialistic, greedy and resigned.

THE ARCHANGEL OF EARTH ★ URIEL

An archangel is an angel of greater than ordinary rank. They possess a stronger, more powerful essence than the guardian angels, through overseeing and guiding the other angels who are said to be with us here on Earth. The word 'angel' derives from the Greek word *angelos* meaning 'messenger'. To humans, angels are often seen as bringers as all sorts of messages. Angels in all their forms are believed to bring the message of 'spirit' into matter, carrying the blueprints of creation and the Source from the Divine into the manifest world. Angels are not and never have been human; they, like fairies and nature spirits, are part of a different evolutionary pattern – but they do appear to us in human form (usually with wings) because that is what we understand. An angel can be in many different places at once, and with the same intensity and concentration, and wish for us to be aware of them and benefit from them.

There are said to be three categories of angels in the cosmos, each with three subdivisions *. 'Angel' is the generic term and also relates specifically to those closest to the physical. Similarly, archangel may be taken to mean any of the higher orders, and indeed signifies the order just above ordinary 'angel'. Found in a number of religious traditions, the word 'archangel' itself is usually associated with the Abrahamic religions. The word archangel is of Greek origin, and means literally 'chief angel'. All archangels end with the 'el' suffix, 'el' meaning 'in God' and the first part of the name meaning what each individual Angel specialises in. The archangel who rules your sign will be the one with whom you most resonate. The astrological sign is an energy signature, a matrix of a specific stellar pattern that will subtly affect and influence you. Although there are many associations for the great archangels of the Universe, we must keep in mind there is great overlapping in their duties and guidance. For example, we may say that one is for healing and another for protection, but they can all perform the functions of the others, and each has only areas of greater focus and responsibilities. Four of the multitude of archangelic beings work intimately with the Earth. These are Raphael (Air), Michael (Fire), Gabriel (Water) and Uriel (Earth). Associated with each of these archangels are one of the four elements, specific colours, one of the four directions or quarters of the Earth, three signs of the zodiac, and a variety of other energies and powers. Understanding these associations and considering them in relation to our own paths, can help us determine with which of them we are more likely to resonate. Your sign, being of the Earth element, vibrates to the essence of Uriel.

* The first sphere, the *Heavenly Counsellors*, comprises Seraphim, Cherubim and Thrones. The second sphere, the *Heavenly Governors*, comprises Dominions, Virtues and Powers. The third sphere, the *Heavenly Messengers*, comprises Principalities, Archangels and Angels. Of course, all such classifications are a human construct, a way of placing order upon the unknowable and allowing us to perceive something about which we have no words to express. However, as long as we think of angelic hierarchies as a way of working with celestials, of remembering important attributes, and we are able to imagine and experience these beings, this order of angels will prove useful to those wishing to draw upon their messages and assistance.

★ ARCHANGEL URIEL'S ASSOCIATIONS ★

Element of Earth
The northern quarter of the Earth
The Summer season
The colours white, burnished gold and all earth tones
The crystals tiger's eye and rutilated quartz
The astrological signs of Taurus, Virgo and Capricorn

Uriel, whose name means 'Fire of God', is the archangel who brought alchemy * to humankind. He is said to be the brightest archangel, a pure pillar of Fire, he can bring warmth to the winter and melt the snows with his flaming sword. Uriel is the archangel of alchemy and vision, overseeing healing, magic, nature and manifestation. This being is known as the tallest of the archangels with eyes that can see into and across eternity. Uriel oversees the work of all nature spirits - working with Uriel will open you to the fairy kingdoms - and works to assist humanity by awakening to them and working in harmony with them. Inspiring us to work with angels, Devas and higher spiritual essences, to perfect our vision of Divine realms, and to refine our mystical nature by burning away our deep-seated desire for comfort and blind ignorance, Uriel is the gatekeeper to the Garden of Eden, the gates of which we can only pass through once we have mastered the wisdom we are given to find our own path to enlightenment.

Alchemy is the sacred art of transmuting base metal into gold by reducing it to the primal black matter and then, by chemico-magical processes, striving to extract and refine spiritual as well as actual gold, the key to finding the way back to Paradise or Source.

TAURUS'S ZODIAC ARCHANGEL ★ SANDALPHON

Additionally, each sign is associated with a particular archangel. Such knowledge can help you to build up a relationship with these beings, based upon your strengths and needs. However, no link is rigid, and as you work with angels you will come to develop your own affinities. When invoking a specific archangel, a useful ritual to draw them closer is to light a candle in that angel's colour, burn some oil or incense of its scent, and hold the appropriate crystal while focusing on what you are needing guidance on.

YOUR ARCHANGEL ★ Sandalphon is an androgynous angel, depicted as a beautiful young man. He is concerned with the spirit behind Earthly manifestations and is guardian of the Earth. Sandalphon stimulates awareness of the Earth's needs, blessings and gifts. Bringing a sense of grounding, practicality and responsibility, Sandalphon can help you be more aware of your bodily power and assist in treating your physical body as a temple.

SCENT/OIL ★ Patchouli

CANDLE COLOUR ★ Deep green or brown

CRYSTAL ★ Jade or brown jasper

THE DEVIC REALMS & EARTH ★ NORTH: REALM OF THE GNOMES

"Through magick we do conjure the Elements, evoking unto us the special properties of the Life-force for our learning and our coming-into-light. And yet are there secret paths of knowledge that have fallen from the minds of men ... For the way of Magick is a path to sacred knowledge, of reverence and humility - and the world is a wondrous place. Yet how many amongst us have fathomed these depths?"
Merlin's Book of Magick and Enchantment, Nevill Drury

Deva is a Sanskrit word that means 'shining one'. Devas are the life force within nature, and there are four devic realms - Fire, Earth, Air and Water - which contain ethereal elemental spirits or sprites.

Elementals are the building blocks of nature, and close to being true energy and consciousness. The four elements correspond to four different states of matter: energy/transmutation (Fire), gas (Air), liquid (Water) and solid (Earth), which are linked to the four human states of consciousness: inspiration, thought, feeling and practicality. There are four spirits, or elementals, which reside in the devic realms, associated with each element. People have been painting pictures, telling stories and writing about these devic realms for hundreds of years, albeit sometimes through disguised mediums such as fairy tales or children's fantasy stories like Tolkien's *Lord of the Rings*. The power of the natural world is easily observed and since ancient times primal forces have been ascribed to various spirit beings. Belief in nature spirits is of such ancient origin and is Universal; cultures everywhere have names or words to describe them. In the sixteenth century, a famous Swiss physician, alchemist and mystic called Paracelsus * defined these beings as 'Elementals', classifying them according to the element of nature they inhabit. There are four main levels of elemental beings: Gnomes (Earth), Undines (Water), Sylphs (Air), and Salamanders (Fire). The fifth element of Ether is the element from which came forth the other four, and Ether, or Spirit, has never been defined in any particular category, and encompasses the aspects and beings of all the other elements.

Elementals are usually benevolent guardian beings or spirits that look after nature's secrets and treasures in whatever part of the natural realm they occupy. They can only be seen or 'felt' by those possessing heightened psychic abilities, yet they can be summoned by those practising alchemy, spells and magic in order to harness the forces of nature for their own particular intentions. In our modern lives, it may seem as though this magic doesn't exist, but the truth is that most of us are simply less in touch with it than ever before. The consequence of this is that we are destroying vast areas of land, polluting waters, creating toxic landscapes, and disrespecting the laws of nature, which often whisper their messages softly. It is therefore important for us to look at the beauty that surrounds us with true appreciation and genuine regard, and to open ourselves up to the magic resides within it. The four devic realms can teach us much about nature; they act as custodians for the four elements, and learning to work with them is a way of attuning to all the energies and beings of nature. Elementals are four-dimensional, and have nothing to obstruct their movements. Therefore, they move as easily through matter as we do through air and space. They do require some contact with humans for their own evolution. Helping to direct them is an overseer, traditionally called the King of that element, and an archangel. Each of these elements is affiliated with one of the four directions and each elemental spirit embodies its own special energy. If you wish to re-connect and re-harmonise yourself by working with nature and its messages and lessons, you could begin by learning a little about your element's realm: Your element is Earth, which is connected with the North direction and the realm of the Gnomes.

* Paracelsus is considered the most original medical thinker of the sixteenth century. His belief in supernatural beings, intuition and the invisible causes of illness helped him discover hydrogen and nitrogen. Paracelsus believed that "Elementals are unlike pure spirits for they are mortal, but they are not like man for they have no soul."

★ GNOMES ★

Gnome: *noun* - A legendary dwarfish creature, supposed to guard the Earth's treasures; diminutive spirits or small fey 'humanoids' in Renaissance magic and alchemy, first introduced by Paracelsus in the 16th century, known for their eccentric sense of humour, inquisitiveness, and engineering prowess; are typically said to be small, humanoid creatures who live underground.

Gnomes are a race of small, misshapen, dwarf-like creatures that dwell in the Earth and often protect secret treasures in vast caverns. Their actions are reflected in the presence of mineral deposits and other kinds of geological formations. Gnomes are the beings of craftsmanship. They are needed to build the plants, flowers and trees. It is their task to tint them, to make crystals and gems and to maintain the Earth so that we have a place to grow and evolve. As guardians of the treasures of the Earth, they are attuned to helping humans find the treasures within the Earth or part of it; this can be hidden riches, the energy of crystals and stones, or the finding of gold within one's life. Ultimately, they work with humans through nature. They give each stone its own individuality and essence. Indeed, they do this with every aspect of nature, and thus we can learn from each one, for every tree, rock and flower has something it can teach us.

According to Paracelsus, gnomes cannot stand the light of the Sun, and even one ray would turn them to stone. If you wish to retrieve any treasures that are buried underground or associated with the Earth, you must first appease the gnomes or they will cause you mischief.

The gnomes are the 'knowing ones', from the Greek *gnoma*, meaning 'knowledge'. The gnomes are the guardians of winter, the direction of the north, the physical world, and of fertility and abundance. The north is traditionally known as the gateway to inner wisdom. The Earth provides us with food and beauty in many forms. The gnomes are caretakers of everything that grows, from tiny flowers to towering trees. The King of Earth is Cernunnos or Ghob, its archangel Uriel, its magickal tool the pentacle or disc (which calls down the spirits into form), and its sacred ceremonial stone is the garnet in all its four colours. Perhaps Merlin sums up the gnome realm best: "From time to time, no doubt, these gnomes do make merry with the lives of humanfolk, having their ways in mischief and making jokes. And yet, for all their pranks and mischief, are these gnomes good and virtuous within their natures, and offer gifts of kindness when hard times come upon our lives."

INVOKING THE EARTH DEVAS

Gnomes are said to be the easiest of the devas to sense since their energy is almost tangible. Earth spirits can be very helpful since they embody practicality and common sense, and have an innate knowledge base around money, the material, and how to grow things. They relate to food, nourishment, health, treasures, fertility, protection, wealth, and all Earth magic.

Gnomes can also assist with the security of your home and are excellent guardians, so it is no accident that many gardens around the world are filled with representations of these powerful beings, as they are said to protect the home they are attached to. Gnomes can also be called upon to bring financial stability to your household, attracting the funds needed to pay a bill or to meet an urgent expense.

If you have a laborious task ahead, have job or financial worries, need to ground your ideals, or are in need of developing a special hands-on skill, ask the earth devas for their help. The easiest way to contact them is to spend some time outdoors around the Earth element and natural features, particularly rocks and thick-trunked trees. You may find it helpful to hold a crystal or stone of resonance when asking the Earth elementals for assistance.

THE NORTH DIRECTION'S CORRESPONDENCES

If you wish to work more with your particular element and direction, the following may help propel your wishes and magical journey:

Time of Day ★ Midnight
Polarity ★ Female, positive
Exhortation ★ To keep silent
Musical Instruments ★ Drums, percussion
Colours ★ Black, deep green
Season ★ Winter
Magical Instrument ★ Pentacle, stone
Altar Symbol ★ Platter
Communion Symbol ★ Bread, salt
Archangel ★ Uriel
Human Sense ★ Touch
Art Forms ★ Sculpture, embroidery
Animals ★ All domestic
Mythical Beast ★ Unicorn
Magical Arts ★ Talismans
Guide Forms ★ Earth, underworld goddess

Meditation ★ Fertile landscapes
Images & Themes ★ Caves, rocks, organic produce, Moon, stars, night, growth and life

HOW YOU CAN GET IN TOUCH WITH YOUR EARTH ENERGY

"The mountain's position is strong only when it rises out of the Earth broad and great, not proud and steep"
I Ching, hexagram 23, ken/k'un

★ Use Earth energy when making wishes around the following: Financial security and stability, material possessions, practical areas of your life, solidity, endurance and stamina, fertility and fertile opportunities, abundance, work and career, home and garden, children, manifesting anything on the physical plane

★ In magical practices, Earth can be represented by soil, salt, crystals and minerals. Earth spells are most powerful when performed outside. A forest, cave or mountain make naturally sacred spaces in which you can attune to the Earth's energy, infusing your work with the forces of nature. Use tools made with materials grown in the Earth, such as clay or stone, salt, herbs, sand, rocks and crystals - and try using a pentagram disc as a base to strengthen the links with your element

★ The best days on which to employ Earth magic are on a Saturday, ruled by the Earthy planet Saturn, or a Friday, ruled by the Norse Earth Goddess Frigg. If possible, choose dawn or dusk when the magical half-light is neither day nor night, a truly mystical time

★ Hike in the mountains
★ Indulge in some hot-stone massage therapy

★ Go camping

★ Spend time outdoors, connecting yourself to the Earth itself - in the form of trees, rocks, mountains and fields

★ Smell a flower, appreciate its fragrance

★ Heal your emotional body with flower essences

★ Red, brown and black-coloured crystals will activate your connection with the element of Earth and will nurture you and enhance healing

★ Exercise regularly, focusing your full attention on your body and its movements

★ Undertake physical activities that enhance your mind/body integration, such as t'ai chi or yoga

★ Learn to love your body

★ Eat Earthy foods and heavy foods which will help ground you, including breads, and rooted fruits or vegetables that grow in soil

★ Aim for greater order and organisation in your life, with regard to time, resources and possessions

★ Cook. Consciously attune yourself to the meals and food you prepare

★ Climb trees

★ Hug trees

★ Lie down in a field of flowers

★ Meditate on the Pentacles suit in the Tarot (the Pentacles suit represents the Earth element)

★ Collect and carry stones, shells, gems and wood, and any other products of the Earth that you find meaningful

★ Study the Earth sciences, such as geology, crystallography or environmental studies

★ Plant, grow and tend your own garden. Flowers, cacti, fruits and root vegetables are ideal

★ Help others learn how to be more realistic, hands-on and practical; as an Earth sign, you are an excellent role model

★ Learn how to make pottery or sculpt using your hands

★ Wear and surround yourself with the colours green, brown and other Earthy tones

★ Cultivate a whole-body sensuality, by giving and receiving massages regularly. You're a natural!

★ Attune yourself to the Earth goddess Gaia

★ Formulate and maintain a regular schedule and routine to help stabilise your energies

★ Devote yourself to finding a home, space or plot of land to call your own, helping to provide you with a foundation and a sense of rootedness in the one place

★ Invest your money in something secure and long-term

★ Surround yourself with friends who are also bodily-oriented and practical; they will help to reinforce and strengthen these facets of yourself

★ When working with the Earth element in magical practice, stand at the North quarter of your magical space, as the North is its domain, and invite its living essence into your 'circle'

★ Earth spirits are also known as fairies, gnomes, tree devas or elves. They provide grounding and attend to emotional healing, so Earth signs would be wise to adopt one (or all) as their very own spirit guide!

YOUR MODE ★ FIXED

Each sign belongs to one of the three quadruplicities, Cardinal, Fixed and Mutable. If we closely examine the Earth's yearly cycle, we can form a very accurate picture of the nature of these quadruplicities, for they correspond directly with the manifestation of the seasons. Each season has three months: the first month brings the new phase of the cycle, the second month brings a concentration of the season's energy to its fullest expression, and the third month represents the transition from the current season to the next one. The astrological quadruplicities represent the three basic qualities in all life: creation (Cardinal), perseveration (Fixed) and destruction (Mutable). Every thing that is born, from a period of time to a human being, experiences a life and then dies. In this context, death can be taken to mean that the form of the energy changes; but the energy itself can never be annihilated, for form is mortal, whereas essence is immortal.

The Fixed mode covers the signs Taurus, Leo, Scorpio and Aquarius, and is the most determined and unshakable of the three qualities. The positive side of the Fixed signs is stability. You are the builders, whether of Earthly creations (Taurus), artistic endeavours (Leo), occult powers (Scorpio), or world-changing visions and ideas (Aquarius).

The Fixed mode signifies the manifestation of purpose and its subjects are concerned with ownership, concentration, stability, fixation, and working with a cool head and calm demeanour under pressure. The Fixed quality is associated with stabilisation, depth, preservation, persistence, loyalty and strength of will. You operate with purpose, dedication, self-reliance and determination, happy to forge ahead, through calmly working away, until you have achieved your ultimate goals. Fixed signs are a fearsome, formidable and quietly forceful group, able to follow their will and demonstrate fixity, often to the point of being stubborn, win-at-all-costs and wilful. Rarely are you distracted in your quests, for you have the ability to stay on firm course and track until a project's end.

You are enduring, deliberate, steady and stable, but may be rigid and single-minded. You have a strong sense of routine, ritual and control. You work hard to consolidate and preserve the things that matter to you, but you can also be inflexible and resistant to change. You stick with situations even when they are outworn, uphold the status quo, and are loyal and dependable, but hate to give in and may lack spontaneity. Your energy and nature is powerful, robust, concrete, limited, set in its ways, purposeful, conscientious, slow, consistent, enduring, stubborn, innately cautious, rigid, unimpulsive, opinionated, unchanging, and you are generally strong in opinions, habits, likes and dislikes. Not easily distracted, you always keep your eyes on the prize, but you have a tendency to brood or to become stuck in a rut. You also project an image of strength as an effective shield against your considerable vulnerability. The Fixed mode indicates the midpoints of the seasons, which are very strong ritualistic times and 'fixed points', signifying points of power in the zodiac.

Because Fixed signs fall in the middle of the season, this term signifies that the season is firmly established - fixed - by the time the Sun enters these signs.

Taurus is the most materialistic and methodical of the Fixed signs, and arguably the stubbornest and most obstinate, with the least fondness for change.

YOUR RULING PLANET ★ VENUS

The Lover, Charmer, Seducer, Romantic & Artist

Planetary Meditation
I am my Earth (my body),
and my Sky (my transcendence)
I am my Sun (my spirit),
and my Moon (my soul)
I am my Venus (my pleasure),
and my Jupiter (my faith)
I am my Mars (my courage),
and my Saturn (my lessons)
I am my Mercury (my thoughts),
and my Uranus (my truth)
I am my Neptune (my dreams),
and my Pluto (my transformation)

Each planet has its own distinctive and original meaning which, according to its position in the zodiac, combines with the qualities that are inherent in each of the twelve astrological signs. If a planet is your sign's ruler, however, it exerts a significant influence upon your life, regardless of its birth chart or zodiacal position.

Benefic ★ Love, Beauty, Harmony, Unison, Pleasure
★ 225 Day Cycle

★ KEY WORDS ★
Love, Beauty, Art, Harmony, Affection, Desire, Relating, Relationships, Pleasure, Acceptance, Social Graces, Vanity, Sociability, Persuasion, Luxury, Unison, Aesthetics,

Outward Style, Indulgence, Refinement, Values, Comfort, Resources, Enjoyment, Agreeableness, Good Humour, Symmetry, Proportion, Mutuality, Sympathy

★ KEY CONCEPTS ★
★ Love, Relating, Harmony ★
★ Beauty in Form ★
★ Social Orientation ★
★ Refinement of Artistic Tastes ★
★ Values & Priorities ★
★ Leisure, Pleasure, Music, Art ★
★ Sentiments in Love & Sharing ★
★ Sensual Enjoyment ★
★ Ostentation & Luxury ★
★ Emotions Connected to Love & Possessions ★
★ Justice & Fair Play ★

Day ★ Friday

Number ★ 6

Basic Energy & Magic ★ Love, Sociability

Colours ★ Light Blue, Green, Pink, Soft Yellow, Pastels

Gods/Goddesses/Angel ★ Aphrodite, Venus, Raphael

Metals ★ Copper, Bronze, Brass

Gems/Minerals ★ Jade, Lapis Lazuli, Rose Quartz, Emerald, Kunzite, Peridot, Malachite (Copper Ore), Sapphire, Green Aventurine

Trees/Shrubs ★ Peach, Pear, Alder, Ash, Birch, Cypress, Fig, Almond

Flowers/Fruits/Herbs ★ Rose, Carnation, Lilac, Pomegranate, Apple

Wood ★ Sycamore

Fabric ★ Satin

Animal ★ Cat, Dove, Sparrow

Element ★ Air

Zodiacal Signs ★ Taurus, Libra

Zodiacal Influences ★ Rules Taurus and Libra; Exalted in Pisces; Detriment Aries; Fall Virgo

"Venus is a woman. At her best, she is what every mortal female might aspire to become and every male to have as his mate. She is capable of any depth of understanding, every height of love. She is the ultimate in beauty of spirit as well as of body. She can show any tenderness, any strength in expressing her love."
Astrology for Skeptics (sic), Charlotte MacLeod, 1972

Venus was one of the five planets known in ancient times. Discovered by the Babylonians in about 3000 B.C., Venus also appears in the astronomical records of several other old civilisations.

Venus or Aphrodite as she is sometimes referred to, was said to have sprung from the seed of Uranus and to have risen naked from the foaming water of the sea, as in Botticelli's famous painting *The Birth of Venus*.

The glyph (or symbol) for Venus is a circle with a cross underneath it, the symbol for the female, and it connotes spirit (the circle) over matter (the cross). Without the crescent of soul of consciousness, Venus is objective. This glyph is related to the Egyptian life-giving symbol, the Ankh, representing the 'mirror' of Venus reflecting our attitudes and values, and is also the biological symbol for female. This image is quintessentially Venus, with its strong associations with grace, desire, luxury, femininity, adornment, love, beauty and harmony.

Venus, named in honour of the goddess of love Aphrodite, is concerned with our relationships and the choices we make in life, both personal and material. It influences the decisions we make, especially when it comes to deciding upon the things and people we value. The mythic Venus or Aphrodite brought fertility, birth, love and passions to all she touched, and through her craftsman husband Hephaestus, she influenced the creation of beautiful objects. She teaches us that contentment and satisfaction are found in nature, in creating and sharing sensual delights, and in giving and receiving affection.

Venus is the secondary feminine principle in our natal chart, the 'female within'. It relates to our urge for relationships, attraction, sensual pleasures, social activities, our sense of beauty, our self-esteem and self-value. It can enhance self-confidence, therefore not only encouraging the *giving* of love, but the *receiving* of it too.

Venus is the planet of love, beauty and pleasure. The signs in which it falls in your birth chart will determine how you express affection and appreciate beauty, and show the sort of relationships and people you attract, as well as your behaviour in love. In a male's birth chart, the position of Venus, a feminine archetype, reveals what he typically projects onto the women he encounters, what he is attracted to in a partner, the qualities he seeks, and what he desires and is turned on by. Venus is his idealised picture of the feminine, his anima, his ideal woman. Venus in a female's birth chart describes a woman's femininity, her image of herself (the hand-mirror), how she presents herself to the world, her desire to look good, what she values in herself and how comfortable she feels with her feminine side. While this is not always true, it reflects how most individuals operate, particularly before one has reached the level of maturity or self-awareness that brings a person to a more balanced inner centre. Perhaps it is an overused cliché, but we cannot receive love from another until we truly love ourselves. There is truth in this concept, and the astrological examination of the planet Venus in one's chart provides the best mirror for this truth.

Venus represents our urge for relationships, artistic expression and tastes, sensual pleasures and that nature of our social connections. It is also about relating, harmony and our sense of values. It shows us how we give and receive, appreciate, and merge with others. While Venus and Mars are the feminine and masculine elements of a chart respectively, this is an oversimplification: desire is the province of Mars, attraction of Venus. Where desire seeks to acquire its object, love seeks to attract it. Venus does not need to exert much effort to attract the things she loves and values; she simply magnetises them to her. however, she invariably always operates in concert with Mars when she sets her heart on something or someone. What Venus wishes for, Mars sets off to attain and conquer for her.

Venus influences our feelings and motivations, and governs our more outer emotional selves. Whether you regard the planets as springs of cosmic activity or as symbols, the astrological importance of Venus is easy to understand. It is commonly known as the *planet of love*, which is an over-simplification, but it does have a powerful effect on our feelings, desires and what we are drawn towards. It also governs how we relate to other people socially and economically and has an influence on our attitude to money and possessions.

Venus is never more than 48 degrees from the Sun, so it either occupies the same sign in a birth chart as the Sun, or falls within two signs either side of it. When it is possible to see Venus, only during the three hours before sunrise or three hours after sunset, it is the most brilliant object in the sky other than the Sun and the Moon. Living up to its reputation for beauty and symmetry, Venus is a perfect sphere, unlike the other planets which are flattened somewhat at their poles. Through telescopes her surface appears serenely smooth, and she has the least eccentric orbit of all the bodies.

Otherwise known as the Morning Star or Evening Star, depending on her position in the cosmos and her relationship with the Sun, Venus can tell us about the type of love we give to someone special. It has been theorised that when one is born with Venus as the Morning Star, she is more untamed, primary, sexual and instinctive in her romantic expressions, and tends to be more impulsive in relationships; they fall in love quickly and without much reflection. When Venus is the Evening Star in one's chart, there is a greater maturity in her gift of love, a greater concern with relationship as opposed to fun and romance. Those born with an Evening Star Venus are not necessarily more successful in partnerships, but their awareness and reflections on love as a deeper transformational process undoubtedly adds a more solid dimension to it.

Venus tells us a lot about how we give and receive affection. In our chart she shows us our socialisation and development, and our relationship patterns/formation style. Its sign is an indication of the qualities that we find attractive and value, whether in another person, a philosophy, an art piece or a landscape. It also signifies our projections in relationships, and the qualities we admire in others. Ultimately, Venus tells us about our urge to love, appreciate and relate, and merge with others.

This beautiful planet is all about appreciation, equality and fairness, our sense of values, aesthetics, our likes and dislikes, and our tastes. She plays a role in our creativity, as she is closely linked with what repels or attracts us, and motivates us to 'create' and artistically express accordingly.

Finances and resources are also ruled by Venus, and she governs money and gifts, as well as sensuous indulgences, such as fine wines, jewellery, gourmet foods, fancy adornments, imported chocolates, perfumes, music and painting. There is indeed a decorative quality about Venus, as well as a feeling of abundance and luxury. As well as opulence and the good life, Venus is associated with fertility, creation and reproduction (her influence coupled with the Moon). Hence the purpose of Venus is to bestow creativity and new life. On another level still, Venus is said to add depth to friendships, strengthen bonds between a child and a parent, and to bring popularity to rulers.

People with a strong Venus in their chart, such as those with a Taurus or Libra Sun, Moon or Ascendant, are social, graceful and friendly, superficial and light-hearted, love pleasurable social pursuits, need others to feel balanced and 'complete', have a well-developed sense of aesthetic awareness, and express affection with ease and grace. They can be the 'hostess with the mostest', possessing all the delightful attributes that make friendships amiable and satisfying as long as the harsher realities of everyday life are kept at bay.

Venus is essentially fruitful and feminine like the Moon. Both rule the gentler and finer emotions of both genders. On their own, they are inclined to be vacillating and lacking in direction and discipline, but given the support of more purposeful influences from other planets in the horoscope, Venusian accomplishments are often wonderful and always artistically pleasing. Venus is known as the 'lesser benefic' after Jupiter, the 'higher benefic', with Venus being more material and physical than her moralistic, loftier counterpart.

Our inner Venus is the part of us that moves to bridge the gap again after a conflict, and has to do with mediating, negotiating and resolution. Too much Venusian influence can result in over-indulgence, superficiality, greed, over-emphasis on materiality, insincerity and promiscuity. These negative tendencies may manifest in destructive ways, unless we can learn to 'allow relationships into our lives rather than taking our lives into our relationships'. It has been said that while women are more likely to project Mars in relationships, men are more likely to project Venus in relationships.

Because Venus rules over two zodiac signs, Taurus and Libra, and both are essentially different (Taurus being Fixed, Libra being Cardinal for one thing), it manifests itself in different ways in each sign: in Taurus pleasure can be found in the Earthly pleasures of material comforts, while in Libra it comes out as a more intellectual approach to beauty, perhaps chic and elegant. Venus's influence in the Libran realm is also more concerned with the interplay of opposites that exist in relationships, and bringing these polarities into harmony. Many astrologers and psychoanalysts believe that we are often magnetised by precisely those qualities that we lack in ourselves, and that we subconsciously choose to incorporate those absent characteristics into ourselves by becoming immersed in them through the medium of a partner who embodies them. However, many people forget why they 'attracted' such a partner in the first place, and then attempt to transform that person into a clone of themselves, or perhaps into a projected idealised image.

Venus is concerned with people's principal desires: love and money. She facilitates harmony between people, connection to luxuries and is generally the planet of good times. She is said to be concerned with our relationships, our values, and the choices we make in life, both personal and material. Venus is happiest when giving of herself as well as receiving affection from others, as she loves to relate, and strives for emotional satisfaction and nourishment. Taurus's energy gives her a sensual edge, Libra's energy gives her an intellectual, sharing and sociable edge. Marriage falls under the dominion of Libra, while the more mundane, practical aspects of Earth life such as food, nourishment, shelter and home, are attributed to Taurus. In Taurus, she shows us our ability to prosper in the material sense, describing how we acquire, use and conserve our resources. In Libra, she lends an energy of social grace, physical attractiveness, and the apparently effortless ability to enjoy good relationships with the opposite sex. However, the downside of Venus in both signs is that you may be inherit her less desirable characteristics, which are self-indulgence, vanity, hedonism, insincerity, low self-worth, superficiality, gluttony, promiscuity (the word 'venereal', pertaining to sexually transmitted infections, is derived from

Venus), or being emotionally demanding in your relationships.

Associated with the things we hold dear to us, Venus is intrinsically linked with sensuality and in short, anything that appeals to the senses, which could include anything from music, art, dancing and movies, to food, sex, exercise and anything else that feels good or enlivens our senses somehow. Because we can be very attached to the things we possess or enjoy, Venus will tell us what we will fight to keep.

Although it is well-known that Venus rules our style of 'give and take' in partnerships, she also has a need to be constantly validated by others to know that she *is* really beautiful and lovely and lovable; after all, she is strongly tied up in our self-worth and value systems - how we value ourselves falling under this umbrella. Generally, Venus in the horoscope addresses issues of self-esteem and how our self-worth holds up or interacts in relationships. One can analyse what makes people fall in love by observing their Venus position, and also what kind of validation or assurance they need from others to bring about their own inner love.

Venus is associated with the pentagram*, gifts, dressmakers, polite, sociable, colour, Friday, holidays, rings, present, cakes, festivities, gentle, music, attractive, flirting, comforts, social affairs, banquets, weddings, duets, caresses, ribbons, adornment, decorations, beauty, honey, money, girls, singing, society, cash, fancy goods, poise, alliances, popular, coalitions, friendship, courtship, ease, gentility, wallets, fashion models, bracelets, lingerie, companions, relaxation, possessions, arbitration, glamour, gains, comrades, candy, mates, boutiques, florists, décor, gloves, good taste, donations, beauticians, wages, gems, social gatherings, concerts, finance, millinery, romance, costumes, pleasure, gowns, grace, leisure, beauty parlours, profits, equality, blossoms, fun, calm, matchmaking, symmetry, flattery, peace, gratitude, sex appeal, bouquets, marriage proposals, greetings, clothes, ladies, sweets, vases, garnishing, rouge, refinement, elegance, etiquette, garments, delicacies, negotiation, cooperation, entertainment, cosmetics, garlands, serenades, flowers, amusement, art, seashells, finery, artists, melody, truces, wigs, brooches, honeymoons, drapes, fiancé, hairdressers, lace, favours, luxury, decorators, pastels, receptions, parties, reconciliation, hairstyles, marriage, songs, oysters, happiness, bonnets, fraternities, sweethearts, embroidery, harmony, celebrations, hats, necklaces, recreation, style, partners, culture, hospitality, toiletries, good manners, confectioners, ornaments, cabarets, affection, pacifists, scarves, emotional attachments, kindness, ballet, diplomacy, dresses, charm, gaiety, furnishings, paintings, fine arts, femininity, tapestries, enjoyment, kidneys, romantic engagements, love, dolls, emeralds, salons, copper, income, interior decorators, intimacy, jewellery, social invitations, lockets, makeup, sugar, orchestras, pacts, suitors, tact and women. I'm sure you get the idea!

This Venusian energy and influence, throughout your whole life, gives Taureans the gifts of grace, equability, an easy going nature, charm, accommodating to others' needs, affection, kindness, friendliness, refinement, appreciation for beauty, aesthetic awareness and placidity. Too much of this Venusian energy can make one vain, lazy, indecisive, weak-willed, dependent, careless, impractical, promiscuous, manipulative, possessive, overly romantic, self-indulgent and greedy. But the Venus-inspired Taurean always knows what keeps her soul in perfect harmony; after all your motto is, "I Possess," and possession of all things beautiful to you, including relationships, gives you all the security you'll ever need. How will *you* use your phenomenally powerful Venusian influence?

* The 'Pentagram of Venus' ★ The pentagram, a five-pointed star, is an ancient and arcane symbol having numerous meanings. Its origins are obscure, but it is interesting to note that in Ancient Egypt all stars were depicted with five points, and one possibility for this is the pentagram's relationship with the planet Venus: the astronomers of the day noticed that every eight years the planet's movements completed the drawing of a pentagram in the sky.

YOUR HOUSE IN THE HOROSCOPE ★ THE SECOND HOUSE

How you spend money is an accurate reflection of what matters most to you and therefore, is a good indication of your whole value system. The Second House deals with how you spend money, what you value, your material possessions, and your overall attitudes toward security, both personal and financial.

A house is one of the twelve sections dividing the terrestrial globe, viewed from a precise time and geographical place, into sectors from the poles to the horizon. The horoscope, or birth chart, is divided into these twelve sections called houses. Each house governs a different area or 'department' of life, such as relationships, career, leisure and even karma. The reason for this division of the Earth into houses can be understood when we consider that the Sun's rays affect us differently in the morning, at noon and at night, and also in summer and winter, and if we study the cause, we will readily observe that it is the angle at which the ray strikes us or the Earth which produces that difference in effect.

Similarly, with the stellar rays, astrologers have observed that a child born at or near midday, when the Sun's rays strike the birthplace from the Tenth House, has an improved chance of public or career advancement in life than one born after sunset. By similar observations and tabulations, it has been found that the other planetary rays affect the various departments of life when their ray is projected through the other houses, and therefore each house is said to 'rule' or govern certain departments of the human life experience.

The Second House, ruled by Taurus, is the house of possessions and assets, personal values, money, self-worth, personal resources, attachments, property and real estate, earning power and spending habits, attitudes towards money and possessions, skills, the acquisitive urge, material circumstances, material security, wealth and expenditure. It describes our ability to earn and retain money, how we earn and spend it, our profits and losses, income levels (i.e. whether they fluctuate or stay the same), the things that we buy for other people, our level of materialism, the prosperity or otherwise that we attract, how 'comfortable' we are, and overall our financial security in life.

Ruled by the realm of the Earth element, this is one of the three Houses of Substance. But where Virgo is concerned with substance on an interpersonal level and Capricorn on a transpersonal and wider-reaching level, Taurus and the Second House are concerned with substance on a personal level. You like to acquire personal possessions rather than those which benefit wider society.

The Second House could be referred to as the House of Personal Values as well as of Money and Possessions, as it reveals a lot about our self-esteem, the attachments we make (emotional and material possessiveness are both themes here), self-preservation, our sense of body awareness, personal security, emotional priorities, how and what we appreciate and desire, our affinity with the natural environment, how and what we value, how much or little we value ourselves, our inner resources, our sensuality and how we enjoy sensual pleasures. It describes what you value ranging from physical possessions and money, to your personal self-esteem, and how you view your own skills and express your talents. What you value and take comfort from, is also found here. This house shows what resources you have to draw on to experience success and fulfilment - potential to be developed. Planets located in this house feel comfortable, and describe those skills, values and attitudes which come naturally to us. As well, it is concerned with security, and reveals how we achieve this; whether or not that security comes from external things that gives a sense of personal substance, or from within, expressed as an inner quality, so that you may live anywhere, in simplicity or with very little, and still feel safe, content and secure. It identifies the strengths that we can call on within ourselves.

The sign and element on the cusp of this house in the birth chart indicate whether an individual seeks security in the tangible or intangible, with Earth and Water signs valuing material, extrinsic, worldly possessions, and Air and Fire signs valuing knowledge, ideas and intrinsic qualities. The sign also indicates whether any financial gain or income is lucrative or otherwise, and whether money comes easily to you or not. It concerns building a foundation and generally *where* we make our income/money. It indicates your financial standing through life and your attitudes towards money - whether you are a spendthrift, generous, a hoarder, greedy, shrewd, or downright miserly or mean. How you use your possessions and financial position to your best advantage is within the realm of this House. It describes your views of money, how you save and budget, and your acquisition of wealth and debt. It reveals much about how you attract and spend your money; and the skills and talents that aid you in generating an income. In addition to relating to your material possessions and worldly goods, it covers items that others buy for you, assistance from others, money lent to you or by you, as well as cheques and financial documents.

Overall, the Second House is commonly known as the 'Money House', and refers mostly to money earned from a job and to portable possessions, one's financial standing, whether or not you live your life amidst wealth, and whether you will labour under misery, obligation or joy. This is where your sense of individuality is reinforced through personal possessions and developed through a solid sense of worth. It is well worth exploring further, don't you think?

YOUR OPPOSITE SIGN ★ SCORPIO
WHAT YOU CAN LEARN FROM THE SCORPION

If we look at the zodiac, we can see that it can be broadly divided into two hemispheres, this division being based on the natural division of the year by the two equinoxes. Astrologers often refer to the first six signs, the hemisphere in which the day predominates (the days being longer in the spring and summer months), as the Personal Sphere of Experience, and the second six signs, the hemisphere in which nights are longer, as the Social Sphere of Experience. These two halves of the zodiac perfectly balance and complement each other, and each individual 'personal' zodiac sign has something to teach its directly opposite 'social' zodiac sign.

To generalise, the signs of the personal sphere tend to experience life through a type of self-projection and self-interest which is often socially uncomplicated, unsophisticated or naïve. Their objective is to learn greater social awareness and thereby integrate themselves with the larger, more Universal human collective. On the other hand, the signs of the social sphere are prone to experience life through the use of their more developed social consciousness. In essence, the personal signs (Aries, Taurus, Gemini, Cancer, Leo, Virgo) usually provide stimulation and new energy to their environment, while the social, more Universal signs (Libra, Scorpio, Sagittarius, Capricorn, Aquarius, Pisces) provide experience, opportunities for wider expression, and give a more broad-minded approach and perspective to their surroundings.

Each sign in a pair seeks and is attracted to the qualities of its complementary opposing sign. Taurus wishes to cultivate the rejuvenated, transformative aspects of Scorpio, while Scorpio seeks the inner stability of the Bull. Taurus dwells within the realm of the collection of *personal* resources and talents, while your complementary opposite Scorpio resides in the realm of the collection of *social* interactive resources and talents.

Although the word 'opposite' conjures up feelings of separateness and differences, the astrological polarities should not be seen as two signs in conflict with each other - their positive expression is to create a natural balance and equilibrium. Each sign has something to learn from its opposite, but also has a contribution to make towards the other sign's more evolved expression. The Second (Taurus) and the Eighth (Scorpio) House polarity is concerned with personal resources versus shared resources, in other words 'mine' versus 'ours'.

These two houses show personal finances, acquisitions, accumulations, possessions and the way in which you relate to other peoples' possessions. The Second House indicates simple personal values, but the much more complex Eighth House shows how these values are projected outward - materially, emotionally and psychologically. In the Second House, the individual produces, becomes attached to and accumulates; in the Eighth House, she destroys, becomes detached, transcends the physical, and spreads herself. Consequently, while the Second

House is related to the instinct of survival and self-preservation, its opposite House is shows obvious similarities with the death instinct, in the metaphorical sense of course. Taurus has not yet learned that to discard something means that a space is then cleared for something new and regenerative to take its place. Perhaps this is something the Scorpio can teach Taurus: to let go of things in order to create a new place for other, more purposeful things to flow in. Taurus often gets stuck in a rut, and is inflexible, unmoving. Scorpio, on the other hand, although a Fixed sign also, is constantly morphing and transforming itself into new forms in order to spiritually unfold. Scorpio can help to turn the stuck, staid Taurean energy around, by teaching the Bull how to open the channels up for elimination and ultimately, restoration.

Negative and Fixed, this polarity is concerned with desire, feelings and possessions. Although you are often attracted to Scorpio, you are also frightened by her fierce instinctuality. Taurus expresses itself with an Earthly simplicity and lacks passion and intensity, but Scorpio can teach you the value of the deeper experience - indulgence, simple enjoyments and creativity can then become passion. Scorpio's intense whirlpool has much to learn from the much less complex Taurus - stability, patience, experience through the senses rather than always through the feelings, natural growth and peaceful, regular cycles.

The balance of this polarity is between the hoarder and the releaser, the retaining and the purging, the drawing in and the expelling, the creation and the elimination. Scorpio merges emotionally and sexually, shares material resources, helps others develop and use their resources, is investigative, penetrates beneath the surface, is concerned with energy and its use, is interested in the occult, gains power through use of emotions and the material, has power over others, is complex, demands that others satisfy her, is healing and regenerating, desires sexual release, is passionate, self-conquering and self-mastering, eliminates non-essentials and enemies, overcomes or sublimates desires, is intense and transformative, and experiences death and rebirth.

Taurus relates to self-worth, material possessions and personal values. It also relates to the doing of everything single-handedly, with a heavy reliance on the self. Taurus has a wealth of inner resources which she wastes no time in manipulating and drawing forth to suit her material needs.

However, Scorpio, dwelling in the realm of shared resources, can teach you how to master *intangible* power, the kind of power which cannot be grasped or held in the hand. She can teach you how to release your Earthly possessions in order to transcend to a higher, more fulfilled way of being. Scorpio's most powerful lesson to Taurus is that material things are not nearly as important as a strong sense of inner personal power.

The Earthy, realistic individual, living through the physical senses and building stability through the simplicity of values (Taurus) seeks to experience the more profound world of feeling which will allow for penetration beneath the surface of things and gain an understanding of deeper realms (Scorpio). The intense and emotional individual, adept at seeing beneath the surface and caught up in the complexities of the underworld of feeling currents (Scorpio) seeks the peace and stability which stems from a realistic relationship with the world and a simplifying of values (Taurus).

Your main karmic goal is achieving regeneration. Taurus is renowned for systematically refusing to change their behaviour. You are deeply attached to and rooted in your routines, values, worldly goods, your concrete life and all the pleasures and comforts within it. Your ideas are fixed and you hold onto them with a stubborn obstinacy, so much so that you get bogged down in your own mistakes. Scorpio teaches you that these attitudes need an overhaul, a reassessment. She highlights the fact that you need to aim sometimes for a complete change, meaning you should strive for detachment, exploitation of inner qualities, and ultimately, for a much greater sense of mental and instinctive trust. Oftentimes you have refused to trust due to fear, but Scorpio tells you that you can release this fear by embracing inner change rather than resisting it. Scorpio knows all too well that the more you refuse to change, the more you run the risk of being forced to do so by the circumstances or events in your life. As well as this, Scorpio intuitively knows that you are very capable of achieving this change.

In order to develop your true highest potential and follow your soul's true path, your soul needs to learn to transcend Earthly possessions and develop a deeper spiritual connection to the inner life force. You cling to things and people in order to feel secure, but to live your life more richly you need to stop placing so much value on material acquisitions and instead work on deeper personal evolution. You need to relax your concerns about attachment, money and security and look at tapping into your phenomenal reserves of power, endurance and resilience. Taurus relies too much on money and physical attachments, but to be your optimal self it is time to probe deeper into what makes your soul really dance. Although you are smoulderingly passionate and sensual, you need to not put so much emphasis on the physical sensation of pleasure but rather how it can further you spiritually. To feel deeper and stronger is your biggest lesson, as you tend to prefer a simple and rather superficial, albeit robust and rich, life. Investigating the darker side of life to find meaning can be confronting at first, but it is something which can help you along your true soul's path and enrich your life with meaning and answers to questions you didn't even know you wanted to ask!

As an analogy, instead of just sipping the wine you so love, really taste it, experience it, feel its passion swirl through you - apply this principle to *everything* you enjoy in life. You need to be more passionate and *feeling* to get the most out of yourself. You also have to go deeper than you may feel comfortable with and immerse yourself more in the complexities of life. Let go of any control and attachment issues and you will rise above your Earthly, possessive existence and soar to much greater heights and dive through wider dimensions than you perhaps currently believe you are capable of.

To evolve to your fullest potential, you need to learn the Scorpion's lessons of expressing the life force more creatively from deep within your heart and thus empower your soul, and in the process stop allowing money and the material world to define you. Your karmic goal is to learn the arts of Earthly transcendence, seeking, releasement, investigating, purging and regeneration. And remember, if you are ever tempted to hoard anything, try hoarding the Scorpio's innate wisdom.

WHAT THE SCORPION CAN ULTIMATELY TEACH THE BULL

Release ★ The path of least resistance, attachments to physical and material goods, your 'comfort zone', attitudes around monetary power, obstinacy, lusty sexual unions, possessiveness, greed, refusal to change, obsessive security needs, fears, carnal desires

Embrace ★ The road less travelled, complexity, greater depth, transcendence, transformative emotions, leaving your 'comfort zone', intensity of expression, empowering attitudes around personal power, inner change, the development of instincts, detachment, Tantric sensual unions, self-mastery, spiritual evolution, shamanistic powers, trust, Divine aspirations

Although moving from Earthly to supernal powers is a phenomenal task, Scorpio is here to help with the transition. Taurus sees the connection between herself and her immediate physical surrounds and manifestations, while Scorpio is aware of the interconnectedness between the self and everything else, not just the physical. Scorpio can teach the Bull how to master inner power and understand the great Mysteries of life; to regenerate and foster greater resilience; to rise above your everyday boundaries and transform others through these learnings; to embrace more fully your powerful inner self; to not allow your external world to define your inner world; to shed your old skin when necessary and rebirth yourself anew; to stop hoarding 'things' and start gathering wisdom; and ultimately, to rise from the ashes after the Fire. While Taurus is scrambling around trying to salvage unburnt physical possessions, Scorpio is busily rising with brand new, brilliant plumage with which she can fly off toward better horizons - completely power-full and unencumbered by money and all the 'things' that would weigh anyone else down.

MAGIC, DRAWING, ATTRACTION, SPELLS, RITUALS, WISHING & POWER

A Note on the Universe

Within each of us resides the merging of the Sun and the Moon, the dance of the constellations, the vibrations of the planets, and the vast microcosm and macrocosm of the entire *Universe*. Uni means 'one' and Verse means 'song'; therefore, the word Universe literally means 'One Song'. If you learn to tune yourself in, you can even hear it!

What is Magic?

Magic is a kind of special energy that is beyond description, and like most kinds of energy it has its own rules and ways of being manipulated. It remains an elusive term, and no definition has ever really found Universal acceptance. Attempts to separate it from superstition, religion and other-worldly phenomena on the one hand, and 'science' on the other, are ridden with difficulties. However slippery the term 'magic' might be, there is a general agreement that most of us wish for more of its presence in our lives and often fall short of achieving this wish.

Those performing spells, 'asking the Universe', wishing, praying, or undertaking rituals, are using this very special energy to draw things to them. Learning to manipulate energy in these ways is never hard (and shouldn't be), but it can be complex and does require knowledge, practice, creativity, patience and above all, imagination. Most of us use simple magic every day, whether by saying little prayers, making wishes, visualising, and exchanging - sending out and receiving - good, positive or hopeful vibes. When you understand that all the forces and magic you need are *within* you, and you learn to *believe* in that power, you are then able to make all manner of changes to your life and, most importantly, yourself.

Magic is an invisible force which connects and permeates everything. Every thought you have and every action you take, will affect the strength of this force, and can be influenced and directed towards a specific purpose by using certain means. The most important of these are your intentions, facing in the direction of your desired outcome, your will and your *belief* that it works. The more you want something to happen, and the clearer you can visualise the desired outcome, the stronger your will and feelings towards it will be, ensuring an avalanche of amazing people, events and circumstances will flow into your experiences, gathering speed, momentum and power as it nears your goal or dream.

The Universe (or whichever higher power you believe in) works for us and through us. Ideas are given to us but they must be carried out *through* us, in the form of asking or acting or performing a ritual or casting a specific spell. The Universe's abundance is your abundance, and it flows through your mind into manifestation. The Universe or Divine Being in which you believe, gives you the necessary ideas and clothes them with all that is needed to bring them into form when we ask *believing*.

Based on ancient human beliefs, systems and superstitions, declaring what you want and acting out your deepest desires can actually help to make things happen. Magical ideas include the notion that thought affects matter and that the trained imagination can alter the physical world, that all aspects of the Universe are interdependent and that we can discover connections and correspondences between everyday occurrences and cosmic, or Divine, energies. A miracle or a wish coming true can suggest something is going on that extends beyond the laws of nature, that something unseen has occurred; but just because we cannot see it or touch it, it doesn't mean it's not there. Magic exists, especially if you truly believe it does, but science is so far incapable of capturing its essence or the rationale behind it. Personally, I prefer to leave that task to the higher powers of the Universe.

To help your dreams come true and to use your inborn power to its full effect, you can employ boosters based on the special energies and qualities of your Sun sign. These 'boosters' are chosen to be in alignment with the purpose of a particular goal, and contain energies of their own which will enhance the strength of your spell, prayer, ritual or 'asking'. Specific magical energies can be invoked by carrying out a spell or ceremony using specific herbs or colours, or on a particular day of the week, according to either your Sun sign (to heighten the power of the asking), and/or that is in sympathy with that for which you are asking (I have included days of the week for other Sun signs and spell types).

Some materials and boosters you can use to increase the power, magic or energy in any area of your life include: candles, wish lists (written on an appropriate piece of paper written with a specially-chosen writing tool), symbols, affirmations, chants, incense, herbs and flowers, locations, colours, days of the week, elements, crystals and gemstones, animal symbols, charms, talismans, amulets, gods and goddesses, essential oils, planetary hours and your Solar totem animals. All are covered, some more briefly than others, for your very special Sun sign to radiate the energy to powerfully draw your wildest dreams towards you!

Overall, it pays to remember that the Universe (or whatever higher power/s or force/s you happen to believe in) creates *through* you that to which you give your attention. What you contemplate becomes the law of your being, and through your pure unwavering belief, is eventually brought through to manifestation on the material plane. What you think about is entirely up to you. But just be mindful that whatever you think about the most becomes your dominant thought, then your main point of attraction, and is ultimately magnified until it becomes your reality or your experience. So choose your thoughts with care. And to quote Ralph Waldo Emerson, "Be careful what you set your heart upon, for it will surely be yours." I carry a copy of this beautiful prophecy in my purse as its words resonate so strongly with me. In other words, be mindful about what you're wishing for, for you will most probably get it, whether it's good or bad - magic, after all, doesn't discriminate. Just make your dominant thoughts good ones, and you will attract everything you set your heart and intentions upon. Good luck!

ASTROLOGY & MAGIC

"Everyone practices magic, whether they realise it or not, for magic is the art of attracting particular influences, events and situations within human life. Magic is a natural phenomenon because the Universe is reflexive, responding to human thoughts, aspirations and desires ..."
David Fideler, *Jesus Christ, Sun of God*

Astrology is the most sublime of the occult * sciences, while at the same time it is one of the most practical for everyday application, for it divines the human soul itself. The cosmos, particularly the patterns that formed across it at the exact moment we were born, indicates the road along which our mental and spiritual endowments are likely to impel us, therefore enabling us to prepare in advance for life's battles, pitfalls, milestones, celebrations and of course to make the utmost of opportunities. Such is the magic of the human mind, that it can 'see' into the future and relive the past without having to be physically present in either, and when combined with astrological *knowing*, particularly the knowing that springs from understanding some of the dynamics of our natal chart, however basic, our inner - and outer - magic can be lifted to phenomenal heights.

In ancient times, not only was astrology the ardent study of the most learned and powerful minds, but among the masses of ordinary people its authority and guidance was accepted and followed without question. How this powerful knowledge was used was - and still is - up to the individual, but all who used it applied it to their perceived advantage.

As primitive humans observed the skies, no doubt they gradually realised that certain stars upon which their fate depended accompanied the seasons, or certain times of the year. They may also have reasoned that if governed their fate, they also governed their bodies, and it is therefore conceivable that the skies were associated with Divine influence. Certain celestial influences were believed to emanate from the thirty-six decans of the signs, and the mysterious but apparent effect that they exercised upon humans were thought to be due to a subtle ether shed by the heavenly stars and spheres on the Earth, that affected not only people, but also other animals, plants and minerals. For the ancient mind, linking magic with astrology may have also provided a much needed sense of predictability and patterns.

Early astrologers named and made associations with the imaginary divisions of the twelve signs and the twelve houses, and people born under a certain sign were said to inherit to an extent, its properties and nature. They also believed that the influence of the planets and stars corresponded with the medicinal properties of certain plants and minerals. They therefore asserted that the influence of a star or planetary position would affect the type of medicine or healing they would offer a subject to attain the most beneficial outcome. Throughout the writings of early philosophers and theorists, there is constant reference to this unmistakable mystic connection between the seven known planets and Earthly affairs and ailments. The seven metals were connected with the seven planets, to which the seven colours and the seven transformations were added. So the alchemist came to share the astrological doctrine that each planet ruled some mineral: The Sun ruled gold, the Moon silver, Mars iron, Venus copper **, Saturn lead, Jupiter tin, and Mercury quicksilver. Consequently, in alchemical symbolism the same sign came to represent the metal and its corresponding planet.

In subsequent years, astrology became closely related to alchemical knowledge and development, and the alchemist came to be regarded as an authority not only on the transmutation of metals, but also on astrology and magic. This goes some of the way to explaining how magic and divination, which had always been inseparably bound up with astrology, came to be associated with alchemy. In all the occult sciences, the supreme power was believed to be in the stars above, and from their mysterious emanations all the metals, crystals, minerals, plants and herbs derived their special properties over time. Further, as alchemy became ever more spiritual and concerned with more abstract and philosophical concepts, eventually it was considered that the transmutation of lead into gold was simply a metaphor for the transformation of base matter, in this case the human soul, into a much purer and higher state of wisdom and being.

The Sun and Moon were believed to have greater influence over the human body than all the other heavenly bodies, and to exert their influence in various ways whenever they entered a certain sign of the zodiac. And although the Moon was traditionally regarded as the most important factor of a horoscope, the Sun has come into its own in later centuries, with the result that almost everyone knows their Sun sign but only those who have delved deeper are aware of the sign their natal Moon falls in. For this reason, I have chosen to focus this book series on the twelve Sun signs, as this is what the majority of people are most familiar with.

The following pages contain methods, energies, materials and objects which may be used to increase the magic and power of your Sun sign's influence upon you. Precious stones, flowers, colours and so on, are regarded as having a potent effect upon good fortune by attuning your mind to receive harmonious vibrations from the astral forces that surround you.

Finally, a basic working knowledge of basic astronomy and astrology is an asset when working with luck, abundance, wealth and personal power. You can attract more of these things when you align yourself with the workings of the wider Universe, the movement of the Sun, stars, Moon and planets and become aware of the correlations between the outer cycles of the skies and the inner cycles within yourself. Also, for those who are knowledgeable about Moon phases, equinoxes and solstices, a world of lucky possibilities can also magically open up to you. You don't need to know about astrology's deepest complexities to understand how everything interrelates; just learning the basics will give you an edge - and hopefully the following lucky tips will provide you with at least a small glimpse into the insights gleaned from your Sun sign, which I am certain will endow upon you the potential for amazing results to manifest in your life - and maybe even a step up one further rung towards the heavens!

* The word 'occult' comes from the Latin *occultus*, which literally means 'knowledge of the hidden'.

** The alchemical sigil for copper represents the metal of Venus. It is assigned to this planet because it is a 'harmony' metal. Copper combines with other metals and, being soft and malleable, it is ideal for artisans to fashion into beautiful objects and adornments.

USING COLOURS, CRYSTALS, DEITIES, PLANTS, FOODS & MATERIAL SUBSTANCES FOR INCREASING POWER & MAGNETISING MAGIC

Alchemist, reformer and mystic Henry Cornelius Agrippa, born in 1486, in his principal work, *On Occult Philosophy*, expressed his belief in the doctrines of astrology and in the theory that the spirit of the world exists in the body of the world, just as the human spirit exists in the body of man. He contended that this spirit also abounds in the celestial bodies and descends in the rays of stars, so that the things influenced by their rays become conformable to them. By this spirit every occult property is conveyed into metals, stones, herbs and animals, through the Sun, Moon and planets, and even through the stars beyond and higher than the planets. A firm believer in the efficacy of charms, he stated that they may "be worn on the body bound to any part of it or hung around the neck, changing sickness into health or health into sickness." I believe the same effect could be applied to wishing and the thinking of positive thoughts, to mean, "Changing thoughts and dreams into manifest reality." He also recommended that these charms be worn in the form of finger rings (that have been created using the materials in agreement and harmony with your Sun Sign's magical energy).

Material substances are connected with abstract purposes by a complex but highly usable and accessible system of correspondences. Use these time-honoured connections in your own spells and wishes to magnetise your desires to you. The following pages will give you some materials, energies, forces and ideas you can summon the power of in order to enhance your magic and luck.

PLANETS

The Planetary influence of the day is important when 'asking' for something. If you are wishing for luck, for example, try working with your Sun sign's inherent energies combined with the perfect day of the week for it. So a Taurean might try using her instinctive money sense, to ask for greater financial luck on a Thursday, which is Jupiter's Day and Jupiter is renowned for being a lucky planet, or better still, ask for luck on a Friday, which is Venus's Day, planetary ruler of Taurus, at the time of day when Jupiter's influence is at its most powerful (information about planetary hours for each day of the week can be found on the Internet or in books on the subject, and can be complex and detailed. It is an art to memorise the correct times, days and energies for the correct spells. If you are determined enough to achieve your dream or goal however, you will be determined enough to put in the research to do it properly!) On the next page you will find a very simplified list of the days of the week and their meanings:

DAYS OF THE WEEK & THEIR POWERS

MONDAY ★ Moon
Cancer

The Divine feminine, changes, intuition, emotions, secrets, dealing with women, purity, goodness, perfection, unity, psychic ability, magic, spirituality, invoking a goddess's or angel's guidance, anything that fluctuates, contracts, increases or decreases.

TUESDAY ★ Mars
Aries & Scorpio

Enthusiasm, competition, passion, energy, courage, protection, victory, anything requiring assertiveness, standing up for yourself, or a 'fighting spirit', determination, vitality, sexuality, self-confidence, men's power, men's mysteries, drive, ambition, achievement, triumph, masculinity.

WEDNESDAY ★ Mercury
Gemini & Virgo

Education, travel, exams, study, communication, making connections, thinking, dealing with siblings, writing and speaking, knowledge, learning, adaptability, charm, youth, absorbing information.

THURSDAY ★ Jupiter
Sagittarius & Pisces

Increase and expansion of anything (remember to be careful what you wish for), luck, growth, influence, worldly power, accomplishment, fulfilment, gambling, philosophy, higher education, abundance, optimism.

FRIDAY ★ Venus
Taurus & Libra

Love, luxury, the arts, indulgence, beauty, marriage, money, prosperity, fertility, women's power, women's mysteries, grace, charm, appeal, hope, pleasure, decorating, self-worth, self-esteem, personal values, business partnerships, romance, creativity, sharing, bonding.

SATURDAY ★ Saturn
Capricorn & Aquarius

Long-term goals, career, institutions, establishments, security, investments, karma, reversal, structure, protection, solitude, privacy, determination, ending, blocking, renewing, transforming, anything to do with the public.

SUNDAY ★ Sun
Leo

All-purpose, success, wishes, generosity, happiness, optimism, spirit/essence, recognition, health, vitality, material wealth, invoking a god's aid or guidance, personal empowerment, spirituality, the Divine masculine.

YOUR NATAL MOON PHASE

Although this book is aimed at enhancing your life through the energy of your Sun sign, a bit of Lunar help can give your wishing a boost! As well as using the planetary days and hours system to add a bit of zest to your wish fulfilment, try combining your Sun sign's power periods with your natal Moon phase (your natal Moon phase can be calculated using a number of sources on the internet, or through an astrologer), or even studying which constellation the Moon is situated in at certain times, to increase the power of your spells and asking rituals. For example, you might like to 'ask' for a promotion at work during a New/Waxing Moon period, particularly if the Moon happens to fall under an auspicious sign for career advancement, such as Capricorn. Your natal Moon phase can also be used to similar effect, by researching when your Moon phase will coincide with a certain Lunar constellation position.

In most astrological interpretations the Sun is regarded as the most important, central feature of a natal chart. But to many the Moon is equally, if not more, important than the Sun sign. Many ancient cultures considered the Moon sign to be more significant. The Moon passes through the 12 signs about every 2.5 days, usually covering the whole zodiac in around 27.3 days. The Moon symbolises our inner world, the world of feeling, emotions, habitual responses, instincts, intuition, security and the subconscious. It describes our nurturing style and needs, our emotional response to life, our attitudes and likely reactions to others, our instinctive and habitual responses, the receptive feminine side of ourselves, our experience of our mother or mother figure, and our childhood experience. It represents the soul. In relationships it symbolises how we like to be nurtured and cared for, and the potential depth of our involvement on personal intimate levels.

For many centuries, people across the world have recognised that the Moon influences the affairs of all living things on planet Earth. The waxing Moon appears to have a drawing, increasing and enhancing effect, whereas the waning Moon has a decreasing, receding and withdrawing effect. All things that come into being are stamped with the qualities of the prevailing Moon stage. It seems that people born during certain Lunar phases tend to share specific attributes with other people born during this same phase. In turn, their attributes will be subtly different from those of individuals born during any of the other stages in the Moon cycle. Knowing exactly which phase of the Moon you were born under gives you all kinds of extraordinarily valuable insights into your character, emotions, behaviour and motivations in life. It can make you aware of your deepest underlying drives, the fundamental purpose that you are drawn towards in life and the contribution you can make to others and society during the course of your lifetime. This knowledge may enable you to intuit and make the most of your own personal cyclical pattern that you go through each month, and allow you to know when the most auspicious periods of time are for you and your affairs, nurture yourself and channel your energies in the most positive directions.

Because this Lunar pattern repeats itself every month, you will find that you can even pace yourself on a long-term basis. This will enable you to effectively target your efforts and goals on periods of time that you know will be potentially fortunate for you. You may in fact find that your birth phase corresponds with the days of the month when you have abundant energy, feel inspired and can generate new ideas with ease. During this period, you should work towards the fruition of your efforts, bring your dreams into light and reach for the stars!

The Lunar Phases Are:

★ New Moon
★ First/Waxing Crescent
★ First Quarter
★ Waxing Gibbous Moon
★ Full Moon
★ Waning Gibbous / Disseminating Moon
★ Last Quarter
★ Waning Crescent / Balsamic Moon
★ Back to the New Moon

SPELLS, MAGIC & WISHING WITH MOON PHASES

Though the Moon has eight astronomical phases, it is the three phases corresponding to maiden, mother and crone that are the most significant in spells, ritual, wish magic and psychic work. By tuning into the physical Moon we can understand and harness these distinct energy phases in our daily lives and magical worlds. The four primary Lunar phases are the New Moon, First Quarter, Full Moon and the Last Quarter. Depending on what sort of spell you wish to perform, your spell should take place during one of these cycles or time periods. Each phase of the Moon is good for some types of magic, but not so much for others.

NEW MOON, WAXING & FIRST QUARTER

In astronomical terms, the New Moon occurs when the Moon rises and sets at the same time as the Sun. Both bodies are found in the same position compared with the Earth. Therefore, a Solar eclipse can only ever occur at the New Moon, when the two luminaries are found, for a short time, in a perfect line relative to the Earth, with the Moon positioned between the Sun and the Earth. The New Moon's sunlit face is hidden from the Earth.

In astrological terms, the New Moon occurs at a time when the Sun and the Moon are found in the same degree of the zodiac and therefore occupy the same zodiac sign, forming a conjunction, or a 'fusing' of energies.

In astronomical terms, the First Quarter occurs seven days after the New Moon. Seen from the Earth, this phase makes the Moon like a crescent, forming the shape of a capital D.

In astrological terms, it occurs when the Sun and the Moon form a ninety-degree angle, or the square aspect, inside the zodiac, the Moon always preceding the Sun.

As the New Moon marks the beginning of a new cycle, it symbolises fresh starts. This is an exceptional time to work magic and make wishes for new beginnings, and for the conception and initiation of new projects. Use this Moon phase for improving health, the gradual increase of prosperity, attracting good luck, fertility magic, finding new love, friendship or romance, job hunting, making plans for the future and increasing your general spiritual or psychic awareness.

Overall, the Waxing Crescent and First Quarter Moon phases are appropriate for spells, rituals and workings that involve growth, healing and increase. This is a period of time lasting approximately two weeks, to draw things toward you and increase things, such as love, prosperity and new opportunities. During this period is the time to bless new projects, anything that requires energy to grow, such as gardens, business ventures, new homes, or educational pursuits. Personal growth and healing are accented, as is 'attraction magic' - drawing something to you such as love, abundance, health, success or a new path - and if done well, you can expect results by the next Full Moon. Magical workings for gain, increase or bringing things to you should be initiated when the Moon is waxing (or New, going from Dark to Full). A time for divination of all kinds, spells of spiritual intention, and for any creative project you wish to see birthed, with magical and fruitful results.

While making a wish within the first forty-eight hours after the New Moon is a powerful way of helping it come to fruition, the most potent time for making wishes is actually within the first eight hours of the exact time of its position. Write down your wish list within this first eight hours on a piece of appropriately coloured paper with a special writing tool, and be sure to capture the essence of your wish by wording it in a way that charges your emotions and simply feels 'right'. Make a maximum of ten wishes (less is perfectly fine too), as making too many wishes might disperse their energy too much to be effective. After writing down your list and releasing your wishes to the Universe in whichever form you feel happy with, keep your list and check on it in a few days', weeks' or months' time to assess whether anything has shifted in the direction of your listed dreams, desires or goals. I'll bet it has - or at the very least, something even better has arrived in its place!

Although the first forty-eight hours after the New Moon is the most potent time to make a special wish, you can begin Waxing Moon magic when you can see the crescent in the sky and continue until the day before the Full Moon. The closer to the Full Moon, the more intense the energies. In fact, a personally devised ritual using any special Lunar-associated materials over three days up to and including the Full Moon is excellent for something you require urgently or within a short timeframe.

In some cultures, people turn over silver coins or jewellery three times when the crescent Moon appears in the sky and make a wish. As the Moon grows, it is believed that prosperity and good fortune will grow too.

While the New Moon is not known as a time for 'banishing' or releasing things we no longer want in our lives, I feel that if we are to ask and wish for things, we need to make room to receive them. Making room means that the Universe can slot it right into our lives where we have cleared our paths for it. Clutter, unwanted things, unhappy relationships, possessions that no longer serve us, are all things we can banish. So, to help what you are asking for come into your life quicker, the New Moon is a particularly opportune time to throw a few things out so you can make way for the new and clear up some space for that which you are wishing for. What are you waiting for? Start creating a space for your wishes today!

FULL MOON

In astronomical terms, the Full Moon occurs 14 days after the New Moon, on the day when the Moon sets at the same time the Sun rises, or conversely. The two luminaries are effectively facing each other, with the Earth in between, the Sun shining its light onto the reflective Moon, giving it the fully lit up appearance of a giant, bright, perfectly round sphere.

Indeed, its entire face is bathed in sunlight. A Lunar eclipse can only occur at the Full Moon, when the Sun, Moon and Earth are all in line, and the Earth hides the lit side of the Moon to us.

In astrological terms, a Full Moon occurs at the time when the Sun and Moon are 180 degrees apart inside the zodiac, and therefore positioned in opposite signs, forming an opposition aspect.

The highest energy occurs at the Full Moon, making this is a powerful time for all manner of magical workings. Use the Full Moon phase for any immediate need, a sudden boost of power or courage, psychic protection, a change of career or location, travel, healing acute health conditions, the consummation of love or a commitment, justice, ambition and promotion of all kinds. This phase lasts approximately 3 days - 24 hours before the exact Full Moon, the day of, and 24 hours after it, according to many sources - giving us 3 full days to perform our spells. However, we are not strictly limited to a three-day period; the power of this phase can actually be accessed for seven days - three days prior to, the night of, and the three days after the Full Moon. The Full Moon period is when the Moon is at her most powerful, being the most luminous and radiant part of the cycle. Known as the 'high tide' of psychic power, the Full Moon represents culmination, climax, fulfilment and abundance. The Full Moon governs all kinds of magic, including manifestation, banishing, and is particularly good for calling forth protection and heightening your intuitive abilities. The Full Moon contains magic that calls forth personal power, fertility, spiritual development, and psychic awareness. Cleansing of ritual tools, crystals, wish lists, Tarot decks, and the like can be done during this phase. Magic worked during the Full Moon often takes one complete cycle to come to fruition. Try also reaffirming your desires during the New Moon to give them an added nudge in the right direction.

LAST QUARTER OR WANING MOON

In astronomical terms, the Last Quarter, or Waning Moon, occurs twenty-one days after the New Moon. The time difference between the rising and setting of the two luminaries is reduced to what it was at the First Quarter. Viewed from the Earth, the Moon resembles a crescent whose lit up area is decreasing in size, forming the shape of a capital C.

In astrological terms, the Waning Moon occurs when the Sun and Moon are positioned at ninety degree angles of each other in the zodiac, forming the square aspect again. However, during this phase, the Sun is instead *ahead* of the Moon.

The Waning Moon represents the Lunar cycle from Full to Dark. Any spells and magic performed during this period is based purely around banishing and releasing. It could involve releasing things which no longer serve you (such as behaviours, material things, relationships and attitudes), banishing negative energies, and removing obstacles which are standing in the way of achieving your goals or dreams. The Waning Moon is the best time for cleansing, gently releasing, eliminating, expelling and completion. It is of great assistance when you are wanting to let go of something, or someone, gradually. The Dark of the Moon, the period when the Moon is no longer visible to the naked eye, until the New Moon, is the most useful time for divination of all kinds.

★ What is your natal Moon phase type? Can you think of ways you can combine it with the power of your Sun sign to effect change and bring about wonderful happenings? ★

HARNESSING YOUR PERSONAL MOON MAGIC ★ MOON IN TAURUS

When the Moon is in your sign of Taurus, it is a great time for working magic around: Money, stability, structure, patience, peace, affection, endurance, material success, and all practical matters. Suggested operations could be around rituals and spells to learn to work with your artistic abilities, savings accounts, and overall harmony. It is an opportune time to work with building your prosperity consciousness, holding onto something you already possess, building and keeping harmony within the home, investing time and money in a project, long-term goal planning, long-term deep healing, and releasing blocks or getting out of ruts. With the Moon in Taurus, you can also seek to cultivate greater patience, more staying power for longer term goals, a bigger bank balance, and to create the underlying structure or foundation for anything (such as a new idea).

THE MOON ★ WHAT IT REPRESENTS IN THE HUMAN PSYCHE & NATAL CHART

The Moon in the sky shines with the reflected light of the Sun. Although not a planet, the Moon is our nearest celestial neighbour and exerts a great influence upon us. The gravitational pull of the Moon affects our body fluids, which contribute to about 90 per cent of our biological make-up. It moves at approximately half a degree per hour and takes an average of 27.3 days to pass through all twelve zodiac signs, staying in each for around 2.5 days.

In astrology the Moon corresponds with the way in which we reflect and respond to what is going on around us. It has to do with our feelings, emotions and instincts and, in the same way the Moon influences the tides on planet Earth, it symbolises the ebb and flow of our emotional nature, our moods, fluctuations and changeability. The Moon is the archetype of the Mother, which is within us all, and represents the primary feminine principle in the natal chart. It is through the Moon that we express our parental instincts - caring, nurturing, protecting, sensitivity. The Moon has links with the past and the subconscious and it is from this almost primitive source that our natural instinctual forces flow.

The Moon is essentially a feminine principle and associates with the inner personality, receptivity, passivity and inward-oriented feelings. It can act as an inner guide to the deeper self, the unconscious self, figures half-shrouded in mystery, linking the hidden personal world of the subconscious to the clearer world of personal awareness.

The Moon is the innermost core of our being, private feelings, habitual reactions and subconscious habits. It is the caring, nurturing sustainer of life, the 'mother' of the zodiac. It tells us about how we seek security, our urge to nurture, our nurturing style, our responses and feelings and moods. The innermost core of our being, private feelings, subconscious habits. It is concerned with habits, mothering, habitual/instinctive responses and personality. It is our karma, our soul, our past.

The Moon represents our mother or mother figure, our feminine side, maternal instinct, our nurturing style and needs, our unconscious self, our emotional reactions, the subconscious, our feelings, instincts, intuition, receptivity, habits, what we need to feel secure, fluctuations, cycles, moods, and our childhood. Its position in the birth chart is very significant, because as well as revealing feminine qualities and the potential gentleness and tenderness of a being, the Moon also reveals important information about the experiences and expression of the five senses.

The Moon is essentially receptive and passive; it reflects the life experience rather than initiating it. Fluctuating and cyclical, the Moon is the planet (although technically a satellite) of the childhood experience, and instinctual reactions. It represents the mother (a child's experience and expectations of their mother), maternal instincts and the feminine principle, indicating how strongly these manifest in an individual, male or female.

As it represents what our childhood experience is likely to be, and childhood is essentially a time where our consciousness has not yet fully developed, our Moon sign traits seem to be more apparent in our younger years. We will usually show our Moon sign traits more so than our Sun sign traits during this developing period of infancy and early childhood, until we have the presence of mind to more consciously develop our ego and true core self (the Sun)

The symbol for the Moon ☽ is a representation of its crescent in its waxing phase from new to full, but it can also be seen as two half circles - these form a bowl shape, a receptacle, a feminine container that 'receives' and 'holds' anything put into it. The half circle, unlike the full circle of the Sun, is finite and incomplete, almost as if striving for wholeness.

The Moon represents our *soul*.

YOUR MOON SIGN

The Sun / Moon Polarity
Conscious & Unconscious, Night & Day, Yin & Yang

> "Man does, woman is."
> **Edward Edinger**

Your Moon Sign, representing your soul, and your Sun sign, representing your spirit, work together to form the foundation of your basic personality, expression and nature. If you know what your Moon sign is, look it up below and read how it works with your Taurean Sun to blend your mind, soul and spirit.

♈ **With the Moon in ARIES, Sun in Taurus**, you are likely to be ★ Devoted, in possession of a robust ego, loyal, persistent, insensitive, greedy, materialistic, self-reliant, self-contained, emotionally strong, bossy, bold, robust, resilient, resourceful, strongly sensual, artistic, enduring, powerful, selfish, pragmatic, firm, in possession of a strong sense of self, stubborn, steadfastly ambitious, competitive, resentful, a powerful leader, controlling, demanding, forthright, direct, irritable, established, entrepreneurial, consistent, steady, possessive, jealous, infantile, a substantial and stable influence on others, irrational, domestic, romantic, generous, practically instinctive, loving, indefatigably resilient, and have an unwavering belief in yourself and your abilities.

Sun/Moon Harmony Rating ★ *6.5 out of 10*

♉ **With the Moon in TAURUS, Sun in Taurus,** you are likely to be ★ Dependable, calm, deliberate, soft, consistent, level-headed, pragmatically intellectual, dedicated, easy going, possessive, stubborn, immovable, supportive, materialistic, nature-loving, certainty-seeking, fruitful, loving, kind, affectionate, slow to anger, in possession of a good business sense, gentle, infinitely patient, slow and steady-paced, security-seeking, tenacious, emotionally placid, rooted, unflappable, devoted, dry-humoured, self-indulgent, logical, stoic, faithful, peaceful, capable, determined, resourceful, peace-loving but strong-willed, reliable, realistic, sensible, persistent, and dedicated to making a substantial and steady income and thereby gaining security.

Sun/Moon Harmony Rating ★ *8 out of 10*

♊ **With the Moon in GEMINI, Sun in Taurus,** you are likely to be ★ Changeable, moody, sociable, friendly, hot and cold, dissatisfied, bright, emotionally versatile, effective, convincing, unsympathetic, perceptive, clever, inspiring, flexible yet stubborn, curious, clear-thinking, torn between freedom and security, practically intelligent, pragmatic, charming, persuasive, brooding, occasionally impulsive, opportunistic, unemotional, unfeeling, conflicted between putting down roots and your need for movement and mobility, logical, creative, progressive, communicative, socially aware, unsentimental, a wonderful friend, a good reasoner, and have a good business sense combined with the persuasive powers of your gift of the gab.

Sun/Moon Harmony Rating ★ *9 out of 10*

♋ **With the Moon in CANCER, Sun in Taurus,** you are likely to be ★ Passive, sensitive, nourishing to others, obstinate, strongly security-seeking, tenacious, retiring, intuitive, emotionally expressive, kind-hearted, tender, sentimental, sympathetic, domestic, resourceful, caring, fertile, creative, shy, emotionally reticent, hidden, private, peaceful, imaginative, poetic, devoted to family, helpful, companionable, emotional, old-fashion valued, self-protective, nostalgic, determined to put down roots, easily hurt, imaginative, sensual, protective of family and loved ones, enduringly loyal, dependable, sustained in approach, supportive, reliable, and in possession of the capacity to translate emotional experiences into artistic expression.

Sun/Moon Harmony Rating ★ *7.5 out of 10*

♌ **With the Moon in LEO, Sun in Taurus,** you are likely to be ★ Proud, individualistic, flamboyant, hospitable, gentle on the surface with a great strength within, dramatic, protective, loving of beauty and the arts, artistic, generous, warm-hearted, gently passionate, persistent, dependable, capable, trustworthy, robust, romantic, affectionate, demonstrative, enduring, noble, charismatic, powerful, honest, snobbish, gently passionate, vain, stubborn, controlling, a leader, wilful, patient, expressive, ambitious, self-centred, vain, creative, comfort-seeking, luxury-loving, helpful, supportive, inspiring, regal, substantial, opinionated, unerringly loyal, materialistic, masterful, ambitious, involved, playful, and in possession of a magnetic, sociable personality with fixed ideas and opinions.

Sun/Moon Harmony Rating ★ 7 out of 10

♍ **With the Moon in VIRGO, Sun in Taurus,** you are likely to be ★ Puritanical, admired, nervous, judgemental, cool, calm and collected, aloof, critical, discriminating, methodical, studious, devoted, hard-working, nature-loving, practical, modest, reserved, helpful, an epicurean, robustly healthy, thoughtful, productive, consistent, supportive, kind-hearted, unassuming, efficient, caring, rigid, conventional, Earthy, constructive, resourceful, efficient, objectively rational, cool-headed, logical, neglectful or unaware of your deeper potential, dutiful, willing to help and do what needs to be done, pragmatic, skilful, reliable, persevering, stable, an artisan, altruistic, humble, wise, lucid, genuinely kind, responsible, poised, and in possession of a good deal of common sense and easy, sensual grace.

Sun/Moon Harmony Rating ★ 7 out of 10 **

♎ **With the Moon in LIBRA, Sun in Taurus,** you are likely to be ★ Harmonious, peace-loving, aesthetically aware, pleasant, devoted, sentimental, attractive, artistic, sensual, able to work with principles easily, sociable, refined, graceful, well-balanced, moderate, easy going, charming, social acceptance-seeking, affectionate, popular, a hider of feelings, approachable, distanced from your true emotional power, sharing, gracious, hospitable, hedonistic, comfort-seeking, pleasure-loving, superficial, romantic, endearing, delightful, gentle, persuasive, artistically sensitive, a practical idealist, and conflicted between self-reliance, self-resourcefulness, and in need of others.

Sun/Moon Harmony Rating ★ 9 out of 10

♏ **With the Moon in SCORPIO, Sun in Taurus,** you are likely to be ★ Intense, bossy, powerful, substantial, robust, highly resilient, inflexible, forceful, subjectively responsive, persistent, committed, charged, resourceful, stubborn, alternating between extreme and mild, possessive, unbending, strong-willed, dominating, sensually passionate, unyielding, sustaining, controlling, magnetic, shrewd, persevering, thorough, hard-working, devoted, dedicated, protective, penetrative, secretive, intensely loyal, emotionally strong, strategic, self-aware, obsessive, courageous, perceptive, self-reliant, exacting, potentially ruthless and manipulative, emotionally powerful, temperamental with a ruthless desire for power, and unshakeable in your ideas and opinions.

Sun/Moon Harmony Rating ★ 7 out of 1

♐ **With the Moon in SAGITTARIUS, Sun in Taurus,** you are likely to be ★ Eager, generous, giving, warm, friendly, idealistic, expressively sensual, big-hearted, moralistic, grounded yet high-flying, adventurous yet conventional, honest, rational, aware of possibilities, inspirational, philosophical, conflicted between freedom and security, idealistic but realistic, prone to preach and boss, able to see the 'bigger picture', distant from your feelings, emotionally reckless, far-sighted, gently optimistic, in possession of an inner knowingness, gently exuberant, a lover of learning, inspiring, aspiring, objective, ambitious, gregarious, broad-minded but rigid, expansive, and guided by reason and logic rather than emotion.

Sun/Moon Harmony Rating ★ *6.5 out of 10*

♑ **With the Moon in CAPRICORN, Sun in Taurus,** you are likely to be ★ Devoted, disciplined, unflappable, dependable, staunch, protective, conscientious, traditional, security-seeking, steadfast, self-controlled, dictatorial, resourceful, committed, driven to succeed, ambitious, reserved, withdrawn, cool, self-restrained, unemotional, wise, shrewd, organised, down-to-Earth, efficient, reliable, organised, serious, sensible, materialistic, introverted, understanding of practical applications and wisdom, economical, practical, honourable, uptight, socially rigid, self-contained, and willing to work long and hard to achieve your goals.

Sun/Moon Harmony Rating ★ *8 out of 10* *

♒ **With the Moon in AQUARIUS, Sun in Taurus,** you are likely to be ★ Friendly, tolerant, objective, living an unusual lifestyle in some way, well-meaning, open to the unusual, emotionally naïve, helpful, opinionated, sensible, artistic, faithful, no-nonsense, unique, sociable, blunt and insensitive when comparing people with your ideals, realistic, committed to principles, inflexible, conflicted between freedom and security, independence and devotion to others, deeply loyal, unshakable, unchangeable, committed to your ideals and loved ones, stubborn, a law unto yourself, and in possession of an approachable, easy going, uncomplicated manner.

Sun/Moon Harmony Rating ★ *6.5 out of 10*

♓ **With the Moon in PISCES, Sun in Taurus,** you are likely to be ★ Imaginative, feeling, warm, loving, romantic, sensual, mystical, idealistic, practically idealistic, good-natured, gentle, intriguing, kind, affable, sentimental, accepting, unassuming, understanding, supportive, strong but vulnerable, a pragmatist, a poet, generous, dry-humoured, generous, receptive, creative, mysterious, prone to drifting and wasting time in daydreams, needy, clingy, impressionable but sometimes unshakeable, quietly strong, modest, practically sympathetic, despondent, impractical, evasive, an escapist from harsh realities, sensitive, perceptive, and in possession of an innate love of beauty, nature and peace.

Sun/Moon Harmony Rating ★ 7.5 out of 10

** If your Moon is in Virgo or Capricorn, your Sun and Moon will form what is known in astrology as a trine aspect. This aspect is the easiest, most flowing and harmonious astrological aspect, ensuring that your Sun and Moon, or spirit and soul, are well integrated. With both luminaries in Earth signs, this gives them the best possible degree of complementary energy - a blending of the elements suggests a balanced expression of personality. One drawback of the trine aspect lies in the fact that its easy flow can be *too* harmonious; if our path is too smooth and difficulties don't arise to challenge us from time to time, we can often become lazy and complacent, stunting our growth and spiritual evolution. As Earth signs, you share the art of practical application, devotion, rational thinking, logic, a love of beauty and peace, determination, pragmatism, sensibility, conservatism, realism, sensuality, fruitfulness and a gentle, caring approach to all your relationships and endeavours, but may be staid, rigid, unimaginative, materialistic, slow, lazy, narrow-minded and lacking in enthusiasm and zest.

YOUR BODY & HEALTH

"A physician without a knowledge of astrology has
no right to call himself a physician."
Hippocrates (born c. 460 BC)

Hippocrates, the fifth century BC Greek physician and 'father of medicine' and supposed author of the Hippocratic Oath, maintained that no one should be allowed to practise medicine who had not first studied astrology. Another Greek physician, Claudius Galen, brought together a huge range of knowledge and ideas in the second century AD which dominated medical practice until the 17th century. Among his teachings was a diagnostic technique which assumed that illnesses and their treatments were affected by and governed by the phases of the Moon. For centuries, astrology was a compulsory component of medical training (and still is in some natural medicine degrees), albeit only one aspect of diagnosis and treatment.

Medical or health astrology concerns particular ways of determining and interpreting an individual's horoscope with particular reference to health issues - diagnosis of current dis-eases, identification of areas of bodily weaknesses, and the prescription of natural cures and remedies. In ancient times, and still even today, the movement of the stars and planets was believed to affect bodily functions, and to cause ailments, or cure them.

During the Middle Ages, many drawings of the 'zodiac man' were made, which showed which signs of the zodiac were related to each part of the body, providing information as to the best times of the year to undertake cures for ailments affecting the corresponding body parts.

Health astrology persists today in many forms and among astrologers themselves, from whom clients seek counsel on health-related issues, and while it certainly cannot be used diagnose a condition or dis-ease, one's Sun sign, along with other factors of the natal chart, can definitely indicate potential problem areas of weakness or possible troubles. This branch of astrology has been found to be surprisingly accurate in most cases. While mostly accurate, none of the following information should ever be used as a substitute for professional medical advice should you be personally concerned about any of the conditions or afflictions listed for your Sun sign.

TAUREAN HEALTH

Taurus is associated with the Throat, Tonsils, Neck, Thyroid, the Metabolic System, the Five Senses, Gums, Middle Ear, Cheeks, Cervical Vertebra, Shoulders, Hypothalamus and Base of the Brain, Thymus, the Cerebellum or Lower Brain, Ears, Lips, Chin, Cheeks, Tongue, Lower Jaw and Vocal Cords. Parts of the body or health concerned with illness or vulnerability are the Thyroid Gland, Carotid Arteries, Sense of Taste, Tonsils, Occipital Area, Jugular Vein, Larynx, Pharynx and the Back of the Head. As a result, you are particularly prone to throat infections, obesity, goitre, laryngitis and tonsillitis.

As a rule, the most vulnerable part of your body is your throat. Infections or a breakdown in your general health will usually appear here first. The neck and shoulders are also weak spots for you, and you have a tendency to suffer from earaches and all manner of throat afflictions.

The typical Taurean is, like its prototype the Bull, endowed with a vigorous constitution and strong health. As mentioned previously, if there is a weak point, it is usually the throat or neck; Taurus is prone to infections of the throat and neck areas, including laryngitis, croup, catarrh, tonsillitis, and swollen glands. Arising from characteristic excesses and indiscretions of diet, accompanied by a sluggish (albeit strong) constitution, constipation may also be a problem for Taurus. When sick or involved in an accident (unusual), you are very robust and can normally withstand any amount of discomfort or pain. Taurus's stubbornness can lead to a determined resilience and refusal to let anything get the better of you. Music and refined surroundings have a profound effect on you, and assist greatly in recovering from illness.

Taureans have a reputation for overeating, its influence affecting the parathyroid, which control the calcium level of the body fluids. Taureans love their food, so can put on weight very easily, creating health concerns if weight gets out of control. A moderate diet is essential but not always easy for you. Thyroid issues, especially low thyroid, weight gain, blood pressure, sore throats, glandular swellings in the neck, sluggish bowels, constipation and haemorrhoids, gout, and tight muscles in the neck or shoulders are very real manifestations of your inordinate fondness for comfort and the good things in life.

As Taurus governs the neck, throat and ears, it also affects the voice (many Taureans have beautiful singing voices), throat area and the lower parts of the head including the chin and tongue, dis-eases that afflict this area of the body, including sore throats and stiff necks, are Taurus-ruled, as are any injuries or wounds which occur in this location.

Taurus's nature is cool, dry and enduring. Taurus rules the five senses and you are a keen user of them. You are a creature of habit and therein lies much of the secret of your continued good health - or otherwise. If your body is subjected to sudden changes in diet or climate, or if you switch from gentle to rigorous exercise, for example, you are likely to become ill. Therefore, you should make all changes slowly, working up to them so that your body has plenty of time to adjust and adapt. If Taureans abide by this rule, they should remain healthy and stable.

Being such a slow and steady character, in most departments of your life it takes you some time to develop an aptitude. You have to practice more than most others and then go over the routine until it becomes a firmly fixed regiment, and after you have achieved this, you are well on your way. Once a Taurus learns something, they never lose it. This is why Bulls can attain high levels of physical competence and timing in sports which require much patience and training to learn, such as trapeze work, gymnastics, acrobatics and the like. Other signs may be more naturally lithe and will mentally grasp a physical discipline quite quickly, but they don't possess your staying power. You master technique in anything usually only through long and arduous training.

Since Taurus is an Earth sign with great natural affinity for the physical body, you usually possess above-average strength. Your constitution is remarkable for its stamina and endurance, and the burdens of work you can carry are extraordinary. Because of this, you are reluctant to give in or admit to an illness. You will go on and on, until you exceed your amazing stamina and have to resign yourself to rest. You won't go quietly, however, and fortunately, because of your powers of endurance, you won't have to rest often. But when you do get sick or injured, it tends to take you longer than average to get back to par again.

You should also guard against any Venus-ruled conditions or afflictions, such as those affecting the following parts of the body or bodily systems, which Venus rules (and many of which it shares with Taurus): Thymus and Thyroid Glands, Venous Circulation, Saliva Ducts, Hormones, Kidneys, Sugar Balance, Hair Shafts and Production, Skin, Neck and the Throat, the Inner Ear, Balance and the Centre of Gravity. Venus is also associated with the Chin, Complexion, Cheeks, Viral Infections, and complaints caused by excesses or pleasures. The veins, venous system, and ovaries may also be particularly weak spots for Taurean and Venusian natives.

Keeping yourself in excellent health overall, with a special awareness of Taurus' vulnerable points, is key to achieving all you set out to do, and getting the most out of your life!

THE CELL SALTS ★ ASTROLOGICAL TONICS

Homeopathy and astrology have colluded to provide a wonderful list of astrological tonics, one particularly suited to each of the twelve signs. These are called 'homeopathic cell salts', 'tissue salts' or 'biochemic cell salts', and are available in most health food stores, are inexpensive and easy to take. They are considered to be gentle, effective and safe, even for children, people in fragile health states, and the elderly. Although the full picture, drawn from a full natal horoscope, gives a fuller, more accurate idea of an individual's unique constitution, even simply working with one's date of birth can be enough for the medical astrologer to suggest the use of a cell salt based upon the correlation with an individual's Sun sign.

As well as the cell salts having a significant effect upon physical ailments, they can also profoundly influence the subtle energy bodies, including the mental, emotional, etheric and spiritual. Although the most common use of these salts is based upon each salt's correspondence with a Sun sign, use of the cell salt related to one's Moon sign can assist with addressing deeper underlying emotional issues, such as anxiety, depression, panic and fear. Use of the cell salt relating to your Moon sign will therefore help to restore your sense of safety, balance, security and emotional resilience. In the first seven years of life, when the Moon is the most influential sphere in our lives, Lunar cell salts are the most appropriate choice as a remedy or tonic.

For specific health problems, take both the salt of your Sun or Moon sign, *and* the salt that pertains to the specific condition. The same principle applies to the Ascendant sign, as the First House represents one's physical health, and especially if the Sun or Moon is a rising planet, which means rulership of the whole chart. For the purposes of this book, however, the cell salt that correlates with your Sun sign only is outlined.

TISSUE SALT FOR TAURUS ★ NAT SULPH.

"Natrum Sulphuricum, or Nat Sulph. (Sodium sulphate) is the cell salt for Taurus. "Nat Sulph. is found in the intercellular fluids (the fluid between each cell) and draws water out of the cells, helping them to break down and be recycled. Its main function is to control and regulate the supply of water in the body, and remove excess fluids from the body.

This cell salt is one of the most important salts affecting the digestive organs and functions, including the pancreatic juices, bile of the liver and the secretions of the kidneys; all are regulated by Nat Sulph. A deficiency of this cell salt can result in such complaints as tiredness upon waking, sluggishness, jaundice, malaria, liver ailments, herpes, kidney disorders, earache, nose and mouth troubles, influenza, constipation and gall stones. Rheumatism, asthma, and other ailments aggravated by living in damp, cold conditions, are also benefited through use of this salt. As Taurus rules the throat, tonsils, thyroid, metabolic functions and the lower jaw, illnesses afflicting these areas occur more frequently when the digestive organs are not functioning efficiently. These conditions can be alleviated or eliminated altogether through use of this Taurean tissue salt.

Overall, its action is recommended as a tonic for the healthy functioning of blood vessels, the liver, kidneys, skin and pancreas. Used with Nat Mur., Nat Sulph. is excellent for any type of watery swelling within the body. Combined with Calc Sulph., Nat Sulph. has a profound effect on the liver. Foods high in this mineral are peaches, spinach, cucumber, blackberries, apple, radish, cabbage, pumpkin, beans, onion, cauliflower, strawberries, celery and pomegranates.

EARTH SIGN TAURUS & THE MELANCHOLIC HUMOR

Greek physician Hippocrates (460 - 370 BC) theorised that certain human behaviours were caused by body fluids, called 'humours'. Later, Galen of Pergamon (AD 131 - 200), a Greek physician, developed the first typology of temperaments to encompass many facets of the human psyche and physiology. These also related to the classical elements of Fire, Earth, Air and Water - as choleric, melancholic, sanguine and phlegmatic respectively. According to the Greeks who developed the temperament theory (the word stems from the Latin word *temperamentum*, meaning mixture), temperament is the 'mixture' of qualities that combine to form elements in physics and humours in medicine. The Greeks sought equilibrium in the four qualities of hot, cold, wet (moist), and dry, the elements of Earth, Air, Fire and Water, and the four humours of choler or yellow bile, melancholier or black bile, blood and phlegm. If balance was achieved, the person was said to be well- or even-tempered, and the importance of determining the temperament allowed for imbalances to be treated.

In ancient times, each of the four types of humours corresponded to a different personality type, which were associated with a domination of various biological functions. It was suggested that the temperaments came to clearest manifestation in childhood, between around the ages of six and fourteen of age, after which they become subordinate, but still influential, factors in our personality. It is important to note that your temperament is not your personality. However, your personality can incorporate parts of the temperament in its expression. Personality is shaped by both external and internal factors, whereas the temperament is innate, an inborn, inherent part of each individual.

The Earth element corresponds with the humour melancholic, which is characterised by long response time delay, and response sustained at length, if not seemingly permanently. Driven by the fear of rejection and the unknown, you tend to be rigid, moody, anxious, sober, pessimistic, unsociable, responsible and quiet.

The melancholic temperament is analogous with the Earth, which is the main element in autumn (or Fall), the season with which Earth signs have many points in common. The nervous system and physical and mental powers reign supreme in melancholic types, although they may often behave in nervous, worried or unstable ways, too. The Mercurial (Virgo) melancholic is distinguishable from the Saturnian (Capricorn) melancholic through the former's obviously more eccentric and less withdrawn mannerisms.

A melancholic disposition represents anxiety, peace and inflexibility. Its taste is sweet and astringent, its nature alkaline, its indication black bile. The melancholic humour is associated with the physical and *solid* body ^, and with cold and dry conditions.

Additionally, the ethereal (or vital) body, comprises four ethers or subtle fluids, which are governed by the four Fixed signs of the zodiac: Taurus, Leo, Scorpio and Aquarius. Taurus corresponds to the *chemical ether*, which rules the basic functions of the physical body - assimilation, elimination, absorption and expulsion.

^ A couple of thousand years ago, the Mesopotamians, Chinese and Egyptians, and more recently the Arabs, practised a medicine called 'of three bodies'. According to the doctors of the ancient world (who often practised as astrologers as well), a human being had three bodies: the physical body, the ethereal (or vital) body and the astral body, imparting a holistic approach to health. In modern medicine, usually only the physical body is focused upon fully. According to tradition, this physical body comprises three principles or states corresponding to three primordial elements: *solid* (Earth), *liquid* (Water) and *gas* (Air). This is the material body, the physical outer cover of muscles, nerves and organs held together by the skeleton. The Fire element corresponds with the *astral* body, which sits outside the physical body in one's auric field.

MONEY ATTRIBUTES

Colour for Increased Earning Power ★ Green

The following plants can be used by all zodiac signs to assist in attracting money ★ Ginger, Allspice, Clover, Orange, Marjoram, Cinnamon, Sassafras, Woodruff, Bergamot, Tonka Beans, Heliotrope, Alfalfa, Coltsfoot, Thyme, Mace, Irish Moss, Clove, Almond, Corn, Honeysuckle, Sesame, Nutmeg, Vetiver, Poppy, Jasmine, Dill and Elder Flower. To attract luck and success, try using any of the above, combined with any of the following: Alfalfa Seeds, Basil, Mustard Seeds, Vervain Leaves, Poppy Seeds, Rosemary, Lemon, Anise and Holly.

Striving for financial gain and abundance with a healthy inner moral compass is, in my view, one of the most noble goals we can set for ourselves. When we have more money, we are better placed to help ourselves and of course others; after all, as Abraham Maslow's Hierarchy of Needs model (1943) attests, once our primary and base survival needs have been satisfied, we can then advance higher towards loftier achievements, such as self-confidence, creativity and self-actualisation. Prosperity allows us to turn our attention to these more transcendental matters - to reach for lives not just of material comfort and luxuries, but of meaning, generosity, balance, harmony, fulfilment and joy. Our Sun sign can offer clues as to how we go about acquiring, earning, saving, maintaining, and allowing the overall flow of giving and receiving money. What's *your* money style?

"The Bull and his money are seldom parted. Not every Taurean is a millionaire, but you won't find many of them standing in line for free soup. Taurus likes to build empires slowly and surely. Oddly, Taurus likes to accumulate power, along with cash, but simply for the sensual enjoyment of possessing it."

Linda Goodman

"Sooner or later, money will come to Taurus, and it usually sticks like glue when it does," Linda Goodman goes on to say. Taureans are very competent financially, know the value of money, and tend to seek secure investments. Rarely fooled by get-rich-quick schemes, Taurus only invests after careful and thorough research. Handling money with care, wisdom and caution is instinctive and comes as second nature to you. However, having a knack for amassing money in the bank and also spending on good-quality and luxury items, you may be prone to greed and over-accumulation.

Taurus, more than any other sign, has an innate and robust sense of money. You put money into bricks and mortar and insure everything. Relating to the Second House of the horoscope, which is connected to the material, possessions, income and security, a substantial and regular income is vital to you. Although you are possessive about most things in life, with money you have a generous heart and open pockets and like to help friends and family out if they are needing help.

You can be protective of your resources and seldom waste money. Careful, controlled, cautious and patient, you're unlikely ever to be wildly extravagant, but do have an insatiable appetite for luxury and comfort, and those things that only money can buy (a cuddle is a lot more wonderful in a country veranda's hammock with a glass of wine). Perhaps your biggest potential downfall lies in being unable to distinguish between need and greed.

You can make money by almost any venture, as you have a natural flair for sniffing things out with your acute physical senses that will increase your stores of ready cash, investments or savings. Farms, land, real estate, art and general finance are all areas that you could benefit from investing in, as you seem to have an instinctive knowledge of each. Conversely, you can also be insecure with regards to finances, as you feel you have to work harder and longer than most to achieve financial stability. You enjoy giving the impression of wealth and are capable of making money work for you extremely efficiently, through putting it into different schemes, and manipulating it shrewdly and successfully.

Usually your money prospects are good and wealth, or at least a steady stream of prosperity, tends to flow to Venusian subjects, whether through your career, investments in luxuries, legacy or a fortunate marriage.

COLOURS

Chromatomancy, or divination by colour, is a form of energy therapy that has been used for thousands of years by many different cultures. It works on the principle that we make both instinctive and rational choices or preferences based on circumstances which are already present in ourselves; colour also has an effect on the energy in an environment, and we in turn respond consciously or subconsciously to our surroundings. If we look at the causes, and try to understand the reasons, as to why we are so receptive to one particular colour over another, we will see that there is a subtle link between certain hues and our emotional and instinctive individual reactions. The colour which we give to things results from a combination of three elements:

1. The light or the vibration of a body;

2. The context in which it is found and the interaction between its own light and that of its environment;

3. The sensitivity of the eye's retina which sees the body in question. Because of this, a colour can vary, depending on the individual's perceptions, namely, his sensitivity, his mood, and his view of reality. For a long time, people have understood that their vision of reality depends a lot on their moods, feelings and emotions.

Chromatotherapy, or colour healing, stems from this body of evidence, and its main application is the use of colours for healing purposes. Colours are generally associated with characteristics, feelings, stones, metals, plants and flowers, planets and even the zodiac signs. In varying cultures, they play a significant role in ceremonies and regalia.

We vibrate to the frequency of colour, shown through its continual movement and change in our aura ^. One of the most beautiful examples of colour is the rainbow. This architect of colour is caused by the refraction and internal reflection of light in raindrops. Colour can be perceived as either a pigment, or as illumination. The colour spectrum can be divided into eight main colours: red, orange, yellow, green, turquoise, blue, violet and magenta. Each colour has a wavelength and frequency that carry different therapeutic qualities which have indirect effects upon our health and bodily systems, and because of this, coupled with the fact that we as living energy centres emanate colour, colour can be a great medium in healing, calming, energising, increasing and attracting.

Aristotle, in the fourth century BCE, considered blue and yellow to be the true primary colours and related them to life's polarities: Sun and Moon, male and female, stimulation and sedation, in and out, expansion and contraction. He also associated colours with the four elements of Fire, Earth, Air and Water. Hippocrates, the father of medicine, used colour extensively in medicinal healing and recognised that the therapeutic effects of a white violet differed from those of a purple one. In the fifteenth century, Paracelsus placed particular importance on the role of colour in healing.

Each Sun sign and planetary body has a specific colour or colours which when used in combination with wishing rituals, can enhance their power immensely. Coloured candles can be used to good effect, as the fire energy of the flame/s increases the power of any wish, and flames are also a useful aid to meditating on, focusing upon or clarifying what you want. Coloured candles help to focus the energy for whatever purpose the colour is in sympathy with (e.g. green for money, pink for romance, orange for joy, etc.)

With all this in mind, wearing or using your Sun sign or ruling planet's magical colour/s on a regular basis will undoubtedly bring great benefits.

^ The aura is defined as an energy field, which interpenetrates with, and radiates beyond, the physical body. Clairvoyantly seen, the aura is full of light, colour and shade. The trained healer or seer sees or senses indications within the aura as to the spiritual, physical and emotional state of the individual. Much of the auric colour and energy emanates from the chakras.

YOUR LUCKY COLOURS

For Taurus ★ All Shades of Blue, Green and Brown, Pink and Indigo - and like a real Bull, avoid Red (except soft shades of Rose). All colours should be subdued and not too bright. Emerald Green is a Taurean colour, and can be balanced with Rose Pink.

For Venus ★ Blue, Pink, Yellow, Green

"The sensuous Bull is tranquillised by the colour of the sky, shades of blue bathe her emotions with peace; also rose and pink, in a lesser way ... The greens and browns of nature calm and soothe her too. Green paper money and a redbrick house will keep her perfectly contented."
Linda Goodman

Ruled by Venus, the first Earth sign of the zodiac has affinity with colours that reflect the principles of Spring, new shoots of life, and harmony - green being the most common. Pink, pale blue and all pastel shades are also colours for Taurus.

Each of the eight colours of the rainbow spectrum also has a complementary colour to which it is matched. Red is complementary to turquoise, orange to blue, yellow to violet, and green to magenta. If these colour pairs enhance each other's most spellbinding qualities and energies, perhaps you could try wearing your Sun sign's lucky colour with its matching complementary colour in order to produce extra magical results! Your lucky Taurean colours are blue, which complements orange, and green, which complements magenta. Now you know your colours, you can dress for success!

FEATURE COLOURS ★ PINK, BLUE & GREEN

★ PINK ★

Planetary Association ★ Venus

Healing Qualities ★ Love, Thankfulness, Tenderness, Joy, Compassion, Romance, Happiness

Keywords ★ Partnerships, Beauty, Friendship, Venus, Friday, Femininity, Soft

Pink is a colour of Venus and is therefore known as the colour of love, affection, femininity, and soft joy. To the eye, pink is a very gentle, subtle colour which imbues one with serenity, balance, peace and tranquillity. The pink palette includes salmon, 'hot' pink *, coral, shell and rose pink, as well as cyclamen, cerise, fuchsia and magenta. Rose pink symbolises romantic love and encourages sympathetic feelings between people generally. It is closely aligned with how you relate to others. This love is not just the love you have for others, but also how you love yourself, with total acceptance and without egotism.

It is considered a gentle colour: deeper shades represent gratitude and appreciation, while lighter shades signify admiration and sympathy. Pink is a romantic and tender colour, that softens the most hardened of hearts and relieves tension. Spaces with pink hues have been found to have a tranquillising effect and reduce the incidence of aggression in potentially volatile or hostile environments, such as prisons. Pink crystals are important in crystal healing, primarily because they bring balance to the Heart chakra, which in turn is your centre of balance. Working with pink gems can also help you deal with the trauma of a relationship breakdown and will help to heal the heart. Pink contains both the Fire and Air elements and is a very useful colour to use in crystal therapy when treating conditions such as anger, anxiety, frustration or fear. Further, it is believed to attract love when used in spells, rituals, and other magical workings: pink candles, ribbons, gemstones and charms, for example, can elicit love when combined with belief and intention.

In Feng Shui, pink is the colour of the southwest and represents marriage and partnership, so is a good colour choice for marital bedroom walls, bedding or decorative accessories; and a pink-painted house is believed to signify marital bliss and may enhance your partnership. It serves two, polar purposes: it represents child-like innocence, but it also signifies flirtation and the potential to lose one's purity. The Taj Mahal in India, the greatest monument to love in the world, exudes a pink aura which confirms this state of being. The gender politics of pink have a convoluted history: initially pink, not powder blue, was considered the traditional colour for baby boys, as it was a toned-down version of the fiercer red. However, in Nazi Germany, pink triangle patches were used to identify and imprison gay men and for decades after WWII, homosexuality remained illegal worldwide. Pink came to be not considered a 'manly' colour. Today, however, the pink triangle has been reclaimed as a positive symbol of the gay community and as such, it represents a culture of inclusiveness, not persecution. If you want to feel supported by Universal love you should wear more of this shade, but if you are feeling overwhelmed or 'fenced in', you should avoid it.

Pink is the colour most likely to reduce stress or to create the 'rosy glow' we enjoy in positive and nurturing environments. It can be used in healing to promote fidelity, friendships, romance, subtlety, and tranquillity. Pink is an overall positive, calming colour which helps to transform negativity, hostility or resentment, into a more vibrant, positive energy at a deep level.

* A trend-setting pink, which was an attention-grabbing magenta, was named 'shocking pink' in the thirties, 'hot pink' in the fifties, and 'kinky pink' in the sixties, and was a fashion leader and bold statement in each of these eras. The colour pink came into vogue through its proliferated use in the cosmetics industry during the sixties - a most defining and memorable decade - when no stylish woman would leave the house without her trusty pink lipstick. At other times, it took back position in the make-up chest and was dismissed as vulgar, sensational, ostentatious and showy.

★ BLUE ★

Planetary Associations ★ The Sun *, Venus

* Blue is said to be the true colour of the Sun

Complementary Colour ★ Orange

Healing Qualities ★ Soothing, Clarity, Calming, Protective, Mental Control, Sedative, Communication, Productivity, Purifying

Keywords ★ Healing, Tranquillity, Thoughtfulness, Peace, Calmness, Water, Venus, The Sky, Truth, Inspiration, Higher Wisdom, Sincerity, Knowledge, Integrity

The colour of Jupiter and the element of Water, blue can be used for healing, clarity, improving perception, protection, sincerity, study and success. Blue has long been associated with healing, calming the mind and enhancing communication. It is the first colour we recognise when we see coloured objects - our eyes contain more receptive cells for blue than for any other colour. Indeed, the largest expanses we see are this hue - the sea and the sky. Blue is cooling, calming and inspires mental clarity and inner peace. It gives us a sense of security and has been shown to lower blood pressure by quietening the autonomic nervous system.

The colour blue symbolises inspiration, devotion, peace and tranquillity, and is a sedating and excellent healing colour. Blue creates a sense of space, so any room or area painted in this colour will appear larger or longer. Because of its calming vibes, it is a soothing and useful colour with which to treat headaches, tension, stress and insomnia. Blue is also one of the easiest colours to wear, it looks smart and sophisticated and there is some shade that will flatter everyone. It has the added value of encouraging focused mental effort and concentration. Lacking in intensity and not making an outstanding impression, it can be nonetheless intriguing and combined with other colours can take on a more dramatic effect.

Many shades of blue take their names from natural phenomena and life forms, for example: sky, ice, teal, peacock, duck-egg, gentian, indigo, cornflower, sapphire and aquamarine. It also has a long history of connections with the Divine - both spiritual and religious. However, blue is sometimes regarded as a gloomy or sad colour, an idea dating back to the 1700s when it was first used in the term 'the blues', referring to despondency or despair. For stress and depression, a colour from the opposite side of the colour wheel can bring additional benefits and offset blue's rather cold nature. Yellow and orange (blue's complementary opposites) are full of cheeriness, optimism and sunshine, and can help swing blue's qualities back towards positivity.

Light Blue is connected with the Throat Chakra and communication; the pure light blue of Italian skies inspired the colour to become associated with the planet Venus and its links with art and beauty and, in its purest form, spiritual aspiration and devotional love. Light blue is connected with the calm of water and the lightness of air, embodying life, refreshment, comfort and femininity. Advertisers use this colour to imply that a product is clean, safe and pure. Dark blue is connected with the Third Eye Chakra and clairvoyance; its darkness has the power to stimulate thought, depth and truth. Wearing darker shades of blue give the impression of reliability, piety and dedication. Royal blue helps to restore self-confidence and to increase levels of mental and physical energy.

Overall, calm, cool and collected blue is associated with thoughtfulness, peace, serenity, water and the sky above, whose pervading energy so affects all who dwell upon planet Earth.

★ GREEN ★

Planetary Associations ★ Saturn, Venus

Complementary Colour ★ Magenta

Healing Qualities ★ Balancing, Harmonising, Calming, Comforting, Relaxing, Soothing, Wellbeing, Freshness, Generosity

Keywords ★ Prosperity, Growth, Money, Springtime, the Emerald City, Abundance, Fertility, Good Luck, Harmony

Green is a colour of balance and harmony; from a psychological perspective, it is a great balancer of the feelings and the emotions, creating an equilibrium between the head and the heart. The most restful colour on the eye, it is the middle colour of the rainbow - a bridge between the colours of physicality and spirituality. Green is the colour of Venus and of the element of Earth. It shares the Heart chakra, Anahata, with pink and when the hues of this energy centre are in balance you feel an abundance of love and happiness. Its healing powers come from its alignment with the natural forces and rhythms of the

Earth. It is the colour of nature, which can reconnect us to planet Earth, and we instinctively lean towards this colour when in need of peace or harmony. Green is also connected with spring, and the abundance of baby animals and seeds sprouting at this time, make it a youthful and playful colour.

Being the colour of balance and sympathy, it has the power to bring the negative and positive energies of a person into balance. Likewise, it has the strength to integrate the right and left hemispheres of the brain, the right hemisphere being intuitive and the left being intellectual. It is also the colour of Spring, of growth, of rebirth and renewal. Green, being such a pervasive colour in the natural world, is regarded as a symbol of peace and ecology. It can be used in healing to promote fertility and beauty. In Feng Shui and other spiritual disciplines, it is said to attract money through its vibrational energy.

As mentioned earlier, Green is the colour of the Heart chakra and bridges the gap between the physical and the spiritual worlds. Opening the Heart chakra allows one to love more, feel compassion and empathise with others. Meditating with a green crystal held over the Heart chakra can help to balance emotions. However, green can also evoke feelings of jealousy and envy when out of balance, hence the terms 'green with envy' and the 'green-eyed monster'. Darker shades of green can also symbolise wealth, avarice and greed. Despite some less desirable connections, this colour works to make your mood more like it: caring, contented, accepting, loving, nurturing and joyful. Green can also balance the three aspects of a person's being, namely the body, mind and spirit, creating a sense of wholeness and integration.

Green is the midpoint colour of the rainbow spectrum, being neither at the hot nor the cold end. It occupies more space in the spectrum visible to the human eye than most colours. Positioned right in the middle of the rainbow spectrum, it gets along well with other colours and can be used alongside them to complement their effects and enhance and brighten duller hues such as grey or brown, rather than overpowering them. Coupled with blue, green is a great stress-reliever and natural tranquilliser. It is not always regarded as a gentle colour; for some, it can signify illness, such as when one's skin turns green if sick, and for others, it has connections with ghoulish monsters, aliens, zombies, vampires and dragons. Also strongly associated with the fairy world, it is linked with elves, sprites, dryads and leprechauns - who can all be very helpful to humankind, but can also be 'impish', mischievous, spiteful and malicious. But despite some negative associations, overall, there is no better colour if you are looking for new ideas or a fresh start, as green is the colour that symbolises and supports growth and natural change. Green is a wonderful all-round soother, balancer and harmoniser, and a beneficial tonic for the mind, body, spirit and heart.

Blue and green, and their respective complementary rainbow spectrum colours orange and magenta, are Taurus's special LUCKY colours! These can be worn or otherwise used together to dazzling and mesmerising effect.

TAURUS'S CHAKRA CORRESPONDENCE ★ HEART

The word 'chakra' comes from the Sanskrit and means 'wheel', disc' or 'circle'. Chakras are vitally important to your physical health, emotional wellbeing and spiritual growth, and are regarded as a complete integrated system that works holistically. The chakras are funnel-shaped spinning energy vortexes of multi-coloured light. These swirling vortexes of energy absorb and distribute life-force, the subtle energy known as *prana*. The seven master chakras - Root, Sacral, Solar Plexus, Heart, Throat, Third Eye and Crown - lie in the centre line of the body, with the first five embedded within the spinal column. Each chakra vibrates at a different vibrational frequency and on a different note, and responds to specific life issues or 'thought forms'.

The lower body chakras deal with physical issues. As we move up the body, the chakras correspond to increasingly spiritual concerns. As a consequence, each chakra's energy vibrates at a different rate, depending on whether they govern earthbound or ethereal issues. The lower chakras have slower and denser vibrations, while the higher chakras spin at faster speeds with higher vibrations.

Because the chakras have no physical manifestation and cannot be located using any scientific instrument, they have tended to be viewed with scepticism by many Western medical professionals, a distinction they share with energy points in acupuncture and the notion of meridians. Instead, they are believed to have been sensed intuitively by many people over many centuries, and indeed people in yoga positions and in deep meditation have reported experiencing the sensation of a surge of energy rising from the base of the spine and emerging through the top of the head. Some people have even said they have seen points of blue light when their *kundalini* energy has risen from the lowest chakra to the highest, as well as experiencing a profound sense of happiness and ecstasy.

In summary, the Universal Life Force enters the body through the Crown chakra at the top of the head. As it works its way through the body, it flows through the other centres. As it spreads to the Base chakra, it is said to arouse the kundalini energy, which yogis believe sleeps in a coiled serpentine form.

The chakra associated with Taurus is the fourth, or Heart chakra, which governs all matters of the heart, namely love, openness, wellbeing and compassion.

HEART CHAKRA

Location ★ Heart Region
Colour ★ Green
Concerned with ★ Love & Compassion
Gland ★ Thymus
Essential Oils ★ Clove, Lavender, Lime, Bergamot, Benzoin, Cinnamon, Elemi, Immortelle, Geranium, Grapefruit, Linden Blossom, Rose, Neroli, Mandarin, Sandalwood, Palmarosa
Animals ★ Antelope, Dove
Shape ★ Hexagram
Element ★ Air

Planet ★ Venus
Zodiac Signs ★ Libra, Taurus
Flower ★ 12-petalled Lotus
Energy State ★ Gas
Mantra ★ YAM

Positive Expression ★ Loving, accepts self and others, innate healer, generous, compassionate

Negative Expression (Blockage) ★ Selfish, envious, jealous, possessive, egotistical, melodramatic, loneliness, lack of emotional fulfilment, difficulty giving or receiving love, lack of compassion, unhealthy relationships, loving too much, unresolved sorrow

The Heart chakra is located in the region of the physical heart. Its Sanskrit name is *anahata*, and its symbol is a twelve-petal green/grey lotus flower whose centre contains a green circle and two intersecting triangles making up a six-pointed star representing balance (six is also the number of Venus, the planetary energy with which the Heart chakra is linked). This chakra blockage is especially significant because it is in the middle, uniting the upper and lower chakras. Among other things, a blockage can manifest as a lack of overall emotional fulfilment and difficulty receiving or being in a state of love. Balance in this chakra is expressed as unconditional love for ourselves and others, as well as openness to give, accept and receive compassion. It corresponds to the thymus and the cardiac nerve plexus. Crystals that can be used to cleanse and balance this chakra are mostly green and pink, such as

Rose Quartz, Jade, Green Aventurine, Rhodonite, Watermelon Tourmaline, and Emerald.

LUCKY CAREER TIPS & PATHS THAT WILL MAKE YOUR BANK BALANCE & SPIRITUAL SELF SOAR

The branch of astrology known as 'vocational astrology' encompasses the areas of one's calling, career path, or ideal profession. Careers, jobs, professions and occupations can all mean different things to different people, but to simplify the definition, I refer to a vocation as one's true calling, one's authentic path, and a dynamic way of life which pays an income in some form and leads to a deep fulfilment of personal and spiritual needs. An ideal vocation will provide self-fulfilment, ego satisfaction, and feed one's inner drive to achieve what they ultimately wish to achieve, whether that be to gain recognition, wealth or approval, to travel, to learn and fulfil an inner need for knowledge, an urge to serve others in some way, or an urge to improve personal, societal or Universal conditions.

In order to gain ultimate fulfilment and self-esteem, we all need a purpose in life. Many people gain this through their work, providing the job or career they choose suits their temperament, talents and aspirations. If our professional life is unsatisfactory or disharmonious in any way, frustration, unhappiness and even despair can result. Although your whole horoscope would need to be drawn up and interpreted in order to gain more substantial, deeper insights into your ideal career and purpose, you can begin by being guided by your Sun sign, which can give you many pointers to a suitable, and therefore successful, career path. You just never know, something in the following might jump out at you and make your soul dance immediately - and hopefully all the way to the bank!

With your Sun in Taurus, you are methodical, patient, affectionate, appreciative of beauty and are a seeker of peace, security and material possessions.

With the gentle sensuality and appreciation of beauty and form that typifies your sign, the world of art, hospitality and physical therapies may hold appeal. In fact, your need for financial security will often dominate your choice of career, so be prepared to take regular breaks whenever you can.

Being one of the most physical and sensual signs of the zodiac, your interests and concerns lie mainly in the realm of the physical senses. You are never afraid of hard work and you rarely shy away from getting your hands dirty. For example, landscaping, gardening, plumbing and drainage concepts are areas of work that you could find yourself in. Many Taureans, especially the men, are physically strong, robust and muscular, making them well-suited for 'hands-on' manual labour such as nursery, garden and crop work. If you are a typical Bull, you are likely to love nature, the outdoors, the simple things in life, and plenty of good, nutritious, natural food. Some of you, being so connected to the Earth, derive great satisfaction from building, mining (especially for precious gems, resources and materials), and bricklaying.

Having a natural 'green thumb', a love of the open air and an appreciation for finances and structure, the following fields may also hold appeal: Building, Finance, Architecture, Surveying, Farming, Banking, Gardening, Horticulture, Landscaping and Real Estate.

As well as having a deep reverence for nature, Taurus, via its connection with Venus, is associated with everything that tantalises the senses, and is beautiful, aesthetically pleasing, colourful, elegant, refined, attractive, decorative, artistic, ornamental and luxurious. As Taurus rules the throat, you also have a resonance with music, and in particularly with singing, or creating sounds and rhythms. There is a long list of fields and occupations which suit those who appreciate these qualities, such as: Artist, Etiquette Specialist, Boutique and Gift Shop Worker, Photographer, Massage Therapist, Gourmet Food Worker, Cake Decorating, Hairdresser, Florist, Painting, Interior Decorating, Jeweller, Craftsperson, Model, Beautician, Confectioner, Fashion Designer, Furnishings Specialist, Milliner, Musician, Resort Worker and Singer.

Having infinite patience, possessing a steady hand and having a keen eye for aesthetics and tasteful design, Taureans also make potentially wonderful tattooists!

As you seek security and stability, your ideal career will be one that is enduring and one that requires consistent input and effort so you can see the tangible results as they unfold. You enjoy the 'fruits of your labour' and luxuriate in not only the completion of projects but the journey also. As you are naturally patient, placid and conservative, you are quite content to work in a vocational field which offers routine and a steady, consistent income. Unpredictable, pressured, deadline-based, or fast-paced work is not suitable for the gentle, unhurried Bull. You will be much happier and healthier in an occupation where you can operate carefully and at your own pace.

Being very financially-oriented, you would get much pleasure and satisfaction in a career which involves dealing with money, and several avenues within the economic field cover this realm, such as Accounting, Insurance, Cashiering, Economics, Property Dealer, Financial and Investment Advice, the Mint, the Stock Market or in a Treasury position.

Overall, a Taurean's ideal vocation would give a soothing, peaceful, unpressured environment, natural beauty, opportunities to work 'hands-on', and the chance to set your own speed.

LUCKY PLACES WHERE YOUR ENERGY IS HEIGHTENED

As the Earth element and melancholic humour correspond with cold and dry conditions, arid but cool places suit your constitution, disposition and temperament. The following nations, countries and cities are also places whose vibrations are closely allied with the sign of Taurus:

Vanuatu, Rhodes, Austria, Tasmania, Russia, Cyprus, Switzerland, Greece, Cayman Islands, Persia, Serbia, the Greek Islands, Cuba, East Timor, Iran, Surinam, Guyana, Rural and Urban Ireland (Dublin), Germany (Leipzig), Capri, Turkey, Italy (Palermo, Mantua, Parma), North America (St Louis) and Ecuador. Guadeloupe, Israel, Jamaica, Mayotte, Sierra Leonne, Tanzania, Yemen, Paraguay and Togo are also in tune with Taurean energy, as are beautifully kept gardens, luxury hotels, upper class restaurants, and rolling, green countryside. Visiting the rolling hills of a sprawling vineyard, anywhere where the food and wine are of excellent quality, strolling through any city's botanical gardens, being spoilt by your loved one anywhere, places that are peaceful and slow-paced and away from hustle and bustle, taking a trip to Australia's Uluru where the powers of the Earth reign and temperatures plummet at night (arid and cool), and indulging your senses in spas, massage, beauty treatments and any therapy which uses the powers of the Earth to restore or refresh your body and spirit, could very well be your ticket to Taurean heaven!

GEMS & CRYSTALS

"People love stones, and apparently stones love people. Like the angels they may be, they seem endlessly willing to serve the wellbeing of humans and to help us achieve our desires ...Unlike people of the ancient past, we now have access to virtually the entire mineral kingdom. We have the opportunity to work like modern alchemists, combining and arranging the stones and their currents, looking for combinations and patterns that can help us enhance our inner and outer lives."

Robert Simmons, *Stones of the New Consciousness*

Each crystal and mineral of the Earth embodies different qualities, patterns or potential expressions of the Divine language, the silent whispers of the Universe. If we can accept the fact that the human body is a sophisticated, multi-faceted antenna system comprised of a crystalline matrix that is constantly transmitting and receiving all manner of energies, it could then be assumed that energy and body workers who use quartz, shells and stones, which are also crystalline materials, have the power to promote resonant interactions with the liquid 'crystal' structures found in human tissues. It could even be said that we are all made of essentially the same substances and structures, and that crystals and gemstones vibrate at varying energetic levels which can connect with our own in order to 'buzz' and dance together to make a harmonious Universe both within and without.

All crystals work through vibrational balancing and by channelling energy. The magic of crystals is in their colour, which is determined by the rate at which their atoms vibrate; these vibrations can be matched to the energy given by your own body's aura. And just as light can be focused and refracted through gemstones, so too can all kinds of psychic energy, from healing energies to Divine communications.

Gemstones can help us attune to higher vibrations and bring them into our own experience and being. This theory of crystal resonance suggests that the characteristic energy patterns emanated by any stone can be transferred into the 'liquid crystal medium' of our bodies through resonance. Our bodies, being composed of these tuneable liquids, can mimic and mirror any consistent vibrational pattern with which we come into contact; we can therefore resonate with the healthful qualities of various crystals and minerals.

Crystals and precious stones have been valued throughout world cultures over many centuries for their healing virtues and capacities to imbue courage, strength, invulnerability, clairvoyance, love and numerous other qualities. Wearing gemstones is one of the simplest and most effective self-healing practices you can undertake, and wearing or carrying those stones whose vibrations correspond with the qualities you wish to embody brings their energetic currents into engagement with your body.

Over time the phenomenon of energetic integration, may be felt tangibly and your own vibrational field may internalise the stone's currents and adjust to them and effectively 'store' them, making them, eventually, a part of your own vibrational make-up. And we seem to know from the resonances we feel within our bodies when in contact with these gemstones, that crystals emanate tangible, if oft immeasurable, currents.

Crystals act as transmitters and amplifiers of your will or intentions - as long as your will or intentions are in sympathy with the crystal's energy. The mineral kingdom refers to stones, minerals and crystals and the associations and vibrations they carry. When working with stones, we are working with several different layers of spiritual energies, and although they can be regarded as inanimate 'psychic batteries', they are actually moving, vibrating masses of energy which transmit potential and power into our lives. Some crystals and stones even have receptive powers, which means they can absorb energy and retain it within until cleansed or re-programmed.

Although it is untrue that the only stones you can usefully wear are the ones astrologically matched with your Sun sign or ruling planet, those which align with your Sun sign or ruling planet are your most fortuitous and therefore strongest 'attractors' and 'amplifiers'.

Twelve oracular gemstones were described in the Bible, as the author of *Exodus* (28-15 and 17-21) knew them. Yahweh spoke to Moses about the breastplate he would have to wear to train for priesthood, and described it to him in these words: "And thou shalt make the breastplate of judgement with cunning work; ... And thou shalt set in it settings of stones, even four rows of stones; the first row shall be a sardius, a topaz, and a carbuncle. And the second row shall be an emerald, a sapphire and a diamond. And the third row an opal, an agate and an amethyst. And the fourth row a beryl, and an onyx, and a jasper; they shall be set in hold in their inclosings. And the stones shall be with the children ... (all) twelve (of them)." Given that the compilers of the Bible lived during a time when astrological belief was prevalent in Babylon, it seems valid to assert that these previously named gemstones would have some astrological basis. Further, since these ancient people supposedly made correlations between each of the twelve precious stones, and one of the twelve zodiac signs, there are seven crystalline systems set down in crystallography (or the science of the laws which influence the formation, structure and geometric, physical and chemical properties of crystallised matter) as analogous with the seven traditional ruling planets of the zodiac.

However, nobody is under the rule of one planet alone. We are all in essence a complex mixture of every planet, many elements and varying aspects, depending on their positions, placements and prominence in our birth chart. Everything that goes on in the skies above us affects what is going on here on Earth, and also *within* us. Your lucky stones are to assist you to tune into your Sun sign's energy and planetary influences, but you are by no means limited to the ones listed for your sign alone. Above all, let your stones, whichever ones you choose, work for you and allow them to transport your very own unique and magical energy into the wider Universe.

> "Beautiful and strong is the material of stones, but more beautiful and much more powerful is the mystery that emanates from them."
>
> **Chinese Poet & Alchemist, Li Po, 8th Century A.D.**

★ CLEAR QUARTZ ★

The Master Healer ★ *For All Zodiac Signs*

A common, well-known and popular gem, clear quartz (sometimes known as rock crystal) is an all-purpose 'jack-of-all-trades' stone. It amplifies the magic of any work you do or wishes you make. It is connected with all the chakras and increases the power of all other crystals. Clear quartz is a deep soul cleanser, which unblocks and regulates energy and emotions on all levels. It is balancing and harmonising. In various cultures, quartz crystal is reputed to be the most powerful crystal, the 'grandfather crystal', and the 'chief of the Stone People'. Clear quartz is also considered to be the only gemstone that is modifiable to suit your needs *, as other crystals automatically contain and retain their own specific resonance or natural signature. In essence, clear quartz is the most easily programmable and the most overall healing and readily accessible crystals of the mineral kingdom, holding a unique importance in the Universe of gems. And because of its all-encompassing nature and wide-ranging healing abilities, it has zodiacal affinities with all the signs.

* To program your clear quartz crystal, simply hold it on your Third Eye chakra (between and just above the

physical eyes) and concentrate on the purpose for which you wish to use it. Be positive and receptive while you allow your crystal to fill with this energy. If you wish, you could also state the intention of the programming out loud, for example, 'I program this crystal for love / healing / meditation / abundance / protection or (insert your own word here)'. You could also run your clear quartz crystal under running water, allow it to dry naturally, then hold the stone with both hands, bring it up to your mouth and blow into it sharply three times in order to impregnate it with your own breath. Then, hold it firmly in one hand and silently invite and welcome it into your life as a friend, helper and guide.

TAUREAN & VENUSIAN LUCKY CRYSTALS, STONES & GEMS

Taurus birth stones ★ Diamond, Sapphire, Emerald

April birth stones ★ Sapphire, Diamond, Zircon

May birth stones ★ Agate, Emerald, Tourmaline, Chrysoprase

Diamond, Sapphire, Emerald (your four primary birthstones), Jade, Rose Quartz (Venusian gems), Zircon, Agate, Tourmaline and Crysoprase (April and May birthstones) are your luckiest stones, and one or more of these gems should be worn about your person to ensure good luck and increase your magnetism. Lapis Lazuli, Coral, Moss Agate, Aquamarine, Boji Stone, Copper, Topaz, Carnelian, Azurite, Chrysocolla, Variscite, Malachite, Kyanite,

Tibetan Quartz, Amazonite, Green Aventurine, Green Calcite, Olivine, Spinel, Titanium Quartz, Selenite, Rhodonite and Tiger's Eye also align with Taurean energy.

CRYSTALS & THE PLANETS

All the Vedic texts agree in relating gems to planets. This verse from the *Jatax Parijat* links each gem to a planet:

'The ruby is the gem of the Lord of the Day (the Sun),
The shining pearl is the gem of the cold Moon,
Red coral is the gem of Mars,
The emerald is the gem of noble Mercury,
Yellow sapphire is the gem of Jupiter, instructor of gods,
Diamond is the gem of Venus, instructor of demons,
Blue sapphire is the gem of Saturn.'

Each planet influences its gem, and their curative power varies according to the position of its planet in the zodiac. Ayurvedic medicine has always paid attention to these details in their healing practices, often advising people to wear their corresponding zodiacal stone as a ring or a talisman.

CRYSTALS & THE ELEMENTS

Crystals are inextricably linked to the four elements, from their original creation to their potency and use in magical rituals and healing. Formed by the combination, in varying conditions, of different physical elements, such as metals, non-metals and gases, some stones require the enormous heat generated by volcanoes or deep thermal currents to bond their molecular makeup, while others may require pressure or water sources. The effects of the four elements of Fire, Earth, Air and Water is evident in these formation processes. The heat generated by Fire, pressure from the Earth, and the chemical reactions involved in absorbing elements from the Air and Water, all demonstrate the four elements in action to produce the correct conditions and ingredients necessary for the creation of crystals, lending them each their unique qualities.

CRYSTALS & THE EARTH ELEMENT

The most obvious elemental force for crystals is the Earth, in which they are found. Crystals are formed over millions of years, which naturally links them with qualities of perseverance, endurance and patience. These gemstones provide the stability of the Earth and the ability to remain, or become, grounded.

Some Earthy crystals are ★ Jet, Onyx, Aventurine, Magnetite, Emerald, Crysocolla, Smokey Quartz, Malachite and Jadeite.

THE CRYSTALLINE SYSTEM OF YOUR RULING PLANET VENUS

Associated with your ruling planet Venus, are Emerald, Pink Coral, Lapis Lazuli, Agate, Beryl, Amazonite, Albite, Pearl, Aquamarine and Light Sapphire. This is the sixth crystalline system, known as triclinical, that is having a parallelepiped on a diamond-shaped base. The stone which perhaps represents this system best, the Amazonite, or aluminium and potassium double silicate, is a brilliant example of it. Analogous with Venus, the triclinical Amazonite had qualities of bringing hope and love to those who wore it.

VENUS'S GEMSTONE ASSOCIATION

★ **Diamond** ★ The Ancient Greeks believed that diamonds were actually splinters of stars that had fallen to Earth, and it was thought by some they were the tears of the gods. Universally considered the greatest of stones, the diamond has been revered throughout the ages for its beauty and strength. The diamond, known as the 'king of the crystals', is a crystalline form of carbon and is known universally as a token of love; quite simply, it is the ultimate symbol of purity. This luminously brilliant gem, through its renowned purity and durability, offers incomparable proof of total perfection expressed in a single element. Its pure white light can help to bring your life into a cohesive whole, the first step in using your power for optimum effect. It bonds relationships, is said to enhance the love of a husband to his wife, brings love and clarity into a partnership, and is seen as a sign of commitment and faithfulness. Psychologically, this precious gem imparts a sense of fearlessness, fortitude and invincibility, for diamonds are unbreakable in every sense of the word. Diamond is also an amplifier of energy and is one of the few stones that never needs recharging or cleansing; in fact, it increases the energy of whatever it comes into contact with and is very effective when used with other crystals for healing as it enhances and draws out their power. However, as an amplifier of energy, it also increases negative energy as well as positive; the merciless light of diamond will highlight anything that is negative and requires transformation. Diamond has been a symbol for wealth for thousands of years and is one of the stones of manifestation, with the ability to attract abundance; the larger the diamond, the more abundance will be drawn to whoever asks for it.

Diamond helps to clear emotional and mental pain, alleviates fear and brings about new beginnings. It also provides a link between the intellect and the higher mind, aiding clarity and enlightenment of mind. On a spiritual level, it allows one's soul light to shine out, cleansing the aura of anything shrouding the inner light, and reminds you of your soul's aspiration; it activates the Crown chakra, linking it to the 'Divine light'. Indeed, clear crystals such as diamond will interact with your energy field by raising your vibration through clearing away any cloudiness or blockages within your subtle bodies. With it may be worn a bloodstone, with which the beneficent influence of the diamond will be greatly increased. Diamond is a highly creative stone, stimulating imagination and inventiveness, and aiding spiritual evolution.

TAURUS'S FEATURE CRYSTAL ★ ROSE QUARTZ

'The Love Stone'

This soft pink translucent stone is quite simply and universally known as the 'love stone'. Unobtrusive though it is, this stone should never be underrated. The minuscule crystals of which it is composed give it amazing durability, and the addition of titanium, a metallic element of profound strength, not only accounts for its agreeable colouring but gives it the power to work wonders on physical and emotional pains and scars. Calming to the spirit and banishing fear and violent tendencies, aggressive energies find it difficult to survive in its presence. It is connected with the Heart chakra and is the stone of unconditional love, enhancing all forms of love and opening up the heart. It is excellent for increasing self-worth and acceptance. Its pink colour associated with Venus, the planet of love and desire, rose quartz is tender and passionate, erotic and nurturing, affectionate and amorous, all at the same time.

Like Venus, this crystal's energies also promote receptivity to beauty of all kinds. Reassuring and soft, it helps to strengthen your empathy and sensitivity. If you have never received love, it will fill your heart; if you have loved and lost, it comforts your grief. Balancing and calming, rose quartz has been used for centuries to heal the heart, attract love, ease emotional pain, foster self-acceptance, treat fertility problems, overcome traumas, and develop a spirit of forgiveness and trust. It is a gentle stone, helping to balance all of the bodily systems and restoring a sensitive of peace and tranquillity; it is an excellent stone to use for bringing harmony to a chaotic situation. It can be placed under the pillow to encourage more restful sleep and ease insomnia.

Useful during stressful, dramatic or traumatic situations, rose quartz can empower you to feel more positive, potent, loving and accepting. Holding, wearing or carrying it also enhances positive affirmations. However, because this stone absorbs negative energies, it should be cleansed regularly if used for healing purposes. It can be cleaned under fresh, running water, then left out in the Sun for a short period to dry. The energies this soothing stone radiates can and should be shared, by giving rose quartz to those in need of comfort a boost of self-confidence and reassurance. Overall, rose quartz has the power to instil infinite peace into your heart. Releasing emotional wounds, encouraging forgiveness and compassion of the self and others, and assisting with all matters of love, it heals and opens your heart on every level, teaching the true essence of love.

TAUREAN POWER CRYSTALS

Around six thousand years ago, in ancient Mesopotamia, the Sumerians started studying precious stones and minerals, as well as the stars, with a view of improving their lives in many ways by probing the secrets and mysteries of the Universe. Their esoteric interests and knowledge were such that they began to grasp the general connections between the Earth and the heavens, or the Solar system as they knew it, and the functions of stones and minerals as a link between the two. Their method of making these connections was by colour (for example the Sun was allocated all yellow stones), as well as other spiritual links. The gemstones listed for the portion of your zodiac sign are given their status as your 'power crystals' due to the links that can be made between your primary planetary ruler/s and your mutable planetary ruler (listed last), and each stone's particular colour, chemical and mineral compositions, healing properties, and the number they are given (based on the Mohs scale of hardness: for example, diamond scores a perfect 10 out of 10), all of which combine to align with your planetary rulers. Working mindfully with your planet's special crystals is one way you can increase the flow of power and magic into your life.

POWER CRYSTALS FOR FIRST HALF
TAUREANS ★ (19 April - 2 May)

Influenced by Venus and Mercury
Emerald, Oriental Emerald (Green Sapphire), Azurite, Malachite, Marcasite Dollar, Pyrite

★ **EMERALD** ★ Emerald is a vivid grass-green precious stone belonging to the beryl family, whose name is derived from the Greek *beryllos*, meaning a green stone. Emerald is mainly blue-green in colour but can also be green-yellow and even yellow. Virtues ascribed to this stone are that of hope, purity, prosperity, love, dreams, kindness, healing, fertility and eternal youth; the ancients believed that it would bestow immortality and good fortune upon those who wore it.

With its dazzling green brilliance, emerald has long been prized for its magical properties and as such has a long history of myth and folklore. Most important of all was emerald's reputation as a link with the Divine forces. It is said to enhance psychic abilities and clairvoyance. The ancients believed that the Greek god Hermes inscribed the laws of 'magic' upon an emerald tablet, and indeed, emeralds were dedicated to Mercury, the winged messenger, by early astrologers. Connected with the Heart chakra, emerald opens and activates this vital organ to heal all problems associated with the heart, whether they be physical or emotional. It is known as 'the stone of successful love' with which unconditional love can be pledged to a partner. By promoting harmony and wholeness to every aspect of one's life, emerald dispels negativity and draws beauty, wisdom and healing to it. Emerald ensures emotional, physical and mental equilibrium and imparts strength of character to overcome setbacks and misfortunes. As a stone of regeneration and recovery, it can inspire a deep inner knowing, broaden vision, and enhance one's wisdom and integrity. It encourages us to follow the laws of nature and, by imbuing us with a sense of beauty and openness, enhances our ability to appreciate the wonders of life. Emeralds were a prime source of wealth in Ancient Greece and Egypt, and this legacy endures today. Emerald is believed to attract good fortune and encourages gratitude, helping you to recognise abundance in all forms rather than just monetary. Perfect sellable emerald stones are rare; most are cloudy or otherwise badly flawed - but whatever their outward appearance, all emeralds can be used for healing purposes. Life-affirming and inspirational, this brilliant green beryl instils a sense of vitality and energy and is an overall uplifting and healing tonic for the mind, body and spirit.

★ **AZURITE** ★ Azurite is a deep royal blue mineral which occurs in small crystals or spherical balls. Azurite was regarded as a sacred stone by the Native Americans, who believed that it facilitated contact with their spirit guides. The Mayans used this stone to heighten their psychic powers, as well as to transfer knowledge and wisdom via the medium of thought and communication. Azurite is particularly beneficial for the Throat and Third Eye chakras and is often called the 'stone of heaven'. Azurite guides psychic and intuitive development and urges the soul toward enlightenment. It stimulates the Third Eye chakra, raising consciousness to a higher level and attuning one to spiritual guidance and unfoldment. Azurite is a vision stone that assists by helping the mind release surrounding chaos and noise which is preventing one from being fully present and effective. It inspires the mind and is useful in meditation, helping to open the flow of the energy systems in the body. It increases focus and sensitivity and allows the higher mind to receive finer vibrations.

A powerful healing stone, azurite facilitates entering a mediative and facilitative state, and enhances understanding the psychosomatic origins behind dis-ease within us (the effect of the mind and emotions on the physical body). Azurite allows us to reach deeper insights by expanding the mind and opening one up to new perspectives. It challenges your old belief systems and releases them, in order to move into the new and unknown without fear.

Azurite initiates purification, renewal and transformational processes, and is good to use with other transcendental stones related to the Third Eye. Emotionally, azurite clears worry, grief, sadness and stress, transmuting fears and phobias. Perhaps most significantly, azurite can open the floodgates of cosmic truth and reveal the essential purpose of your life to you. It is a stone for highly evolved souls, and many find it an aid to their psychic development, but will also discover that its effects are short-lived. This stone also has the peculiar quality of slowly but inexorably morphing from royal blue and into another mineral, the deep green malachite. During its working life as azurite, however, it frees channels along which its wearers might fear to tread. As malachite, this stone has physical healing properties as well as emotional. But as azurite, it seems to operate almost entirely on the spiritual level alone.

★ **MALACHITE** * ★ Malachite is a striking, rich-green layered opaque stone of intense energy. Its dramatic patterns echo its versatile and vast healing qualities. It is so named because its layers resemble the soft green of the marshmallow plant, derived from the Greek word for the plant's colouring - *malache*. It is connected with the Solar Plexus, Throat and Heart chakras, and although powerful and probing, it will increase courage and determination, dissolving fear and anxiety, and help you break free from limitations. Malachite is a copper-rich crystal which can be used diagnostically to get to the heart of a problem. It is a stone of balance that soothes, but also strengthens, the nervous system. A resolute stone that draws insights out from deep within the subconscious mind and facilitates the regeneration of the self, with dedicated use, this intense stone can balance and bring harmony to the body and psyche.

Malachite is an exceptionally evolving ** stone that is perfect for all self-transformational explorations, and the more you work with it, the more expansive its influence becomes. It illuminates the darker corners of the mind, and in doing so demands that you examine the deep-rooted causes of any physical or mental issues. This is also a stone of alignment and is excellent to use in self-exploration journeys. Working with malachite ultimately helps you confront whatever it is that is blocking your spiritual unfolding and wellbeing. It also has a detoxifying effect, cleansing the body of both physical and emotional impurities. Assisting in the release of outworn or restrictive patterns of thought or behaviour, it is both physically and psychologically vitalising. It also facilitates release and letting go, enabling you to move forward. Used in combination with other similarly acting crystals, malachite can heal grief, ease heartache, draw out toxic emotions, break unwanted ties, root out psychosomatic causes of bodily dis-ease, and teach you how to take responsibility for your thoughts, actions and feelings.

Malachite is known as the 'sleep stone' because it has the effect of inducing drowsiness if gazed at for long enough. It can ease insomnia, improve quality of sleep and dreaming, and offer protection from nightmares. Malachite is used for its protective properties as well. It absorbs pollutants and negative energies, picking them up from the atmosphere, the physical body and the aura. It guards against radiation of all kinds and soaks up plutonium pollution. It also clears electromagnetic pollution and heals Earth energies. Malachite can be used for scrying - journeying through its convoluted patterns can stimulate pictures, and assist in receiving insights or messages from the future. It is regarded as "the mirror of the soul" and so some crystal experts may advise against wearing malachite as it may prove too powerful and confronting for some. Essentially, it is a true empowerment crystal, which helps you reclaim your power by bringing to the surface any hidden issues, toxic thoughts or repressed feelings that are holding you back. If this stone had an expression, it would be, "I Am." It will help those who are brave enough to work with it, to step into your true power.

As a stone of transformation and change, life is lived more intensely and adventurously under the influence of this vivid gem. It will enhance spiritual rebirth and growth and when placed on the Solar Plexus it will facilitate deep emotional healing, allowing one's deepest self to shift in a new, positive direction. This intense crystal will surprise you with its merciless spotlight on what has held you back for so long - and will further astound with the depth of transmutation that you can achieve with it.

* Malachite will lose its sheen if cleansed in salt water - smudging this crystal with sandalwood or sage incense is preferable. It should be cleansed before and after use by placing it on a quartz cluster in the Sun. Also, malachite needs to be handled with caution and is best used under the supervision of a qualified crystal therapist. Always use malachite in its polished form, and wash your hands after use.

** It is believed by some people that malachite is still evolving and will be one of the most important healing stones in years to come.

★ **PYRITE** ★ Pyrite, or iron pyrite, is an earthy metallic crystal associated with the Earth element, to help bring forth its riches and to promote the fertility and good fortune of a project or to boost your own financial investments. Also known as fool's gold, Inca stone and fire stone *, pyrite often appears as a beautiful golden mineral that has fooled many a prospector in their quest for the real thing. Pyrite has its place in modern day science and alchemy also, being used as a good source of sulphuric acid by scientists and alchemists for the last 1,000 years.

Lapis lazuli, an enchanting deep blue stone with gold 'flecks', contains pyrite, as do other crystals such as praziolite and schorl. A piece of pyrite placed on a desk energises the area around it. It is helpful when planning large business concepts, by helping one tap into one's ability and potential and stimulating the flow of ideas. It is also believed to attract prosperity. Pyrite is essentially a brassy, silver to gold-coloured iron mineral which occurs in clusters, chunks, cubes, and more rarely as flat, circular plates often called 'Suns' or 'sand dollars'. Pyrite works well with all the chakras and makes a good companion for amethyst in the development of spiritual vision and psychic abilities. Used at the Third Eye, it will help this development. As a stone that enhances concentration and memory, it will help ground any spiritual or psychic insights amethyst gives rise to, and imprint these understandings on your cellular memory. Mental activity is accelerated by pyrite as it increases blood flow to the brain.

Pyrite resonates with the energies of the Sun and is joyous and uplifting. It can be used at the Solar Plexus chakra for the purpose of enhancing personal and psychic power and to transmit thought-forms to another or to the Universe. It can also be used at the Base and Crown chakras simultaneously to open the chakras and to ground the information received. Pyrite also possesses protective qualities, protecting against negative influences and evil energies, sending them back to their source. Psychologically, pyrite relieves anxiety, melancholy, deep despair and frustration and boosts self-worth and confidence. Associated with the blood, eyes and brain, it can promote cleansing and healing of all these areas. To best ensure the success of pyrite's positive properties, position them where they can soak up the powerful and energising light of the Sun.

* Pyrite is also known as fire stone, because it gives off sparks when struck with a hard object. This makes it a potential fire hazard in mines. For this reason, combined with its often mistaken identity for real gold, pyrite is disliked by miners.

POWER CRYSTALS FOR SECOND HALF TAUREANS ★ (3 - 19 May)

Influenced by Venus and Saturn

Andalusite, Chiastolite, Sphalerite, Lavender Jadeite, Pyritised Ammonite, Irish Fairy Stone

★ **CHIASTOLITE** ★ Chiastolite is a powerfully protective stone with a distinctive cross in its centre when polished. Chiastolite is an excellent crystal for maintaining one's spirituality when faced with mortality and leaving the physical plane, or passing over - it will assist in making a smooth transition. It is a creative stone which has the properties of transmuting disharmony into harmony and the power to dispel negative thoughts and feelings. Chiastolite assists out-of-body journeying and provides a gateway into - and answers about - mysteries. A stone that promotes change, it dissolves illusions and calms fears, enabling you to face reality and aiding in the transition between one situation and another, especially at the psychological level. Chiastolite helps to clear away feelings of guilt, releases worn out patterns and conditioning, and invokes protective forces. It stabilises the emotions and assists with problem-solving and insight, clearing the way so that you can attune to your soul's purpose.

★ **LAVENDER JADEITE** ★ Lavender jadeite is a pale pinkish purple stone which emanates pure energy of the highest etheric spectrum. It provides spiritual nourishment, is excellent for meditation, and helps one to embrace an attitude of serene acceptance. In addition to the generic attributes of jade, lavender jadeite (or jade) alleviates emotional hurt and trauma, releases cynicism and bestows inner peace. Its higher guidance and connection with the cosmic and etheric planes expands emotional awareness and encourages empathy. It teaches subtlety and restraint in emotional matters, holds back the excessive expression of feelings, and helps to set clear boundaries.

Lavender jadeite, like its better known 'sister' green jade, has an affinity for the Heart chakra, and both open up the heart on an emotional, as well as physical level. Physically, jade is used for deepening the breathing and treating heart problems in general, while emotionally it encourages compassion and the establishment of strong bonds. Lavender jade balances the nervous system, dispelling mood swings and calming anger and irritability. It is also useful as a dream stone: a piece placed under your pillow will enable you to both remember and to interpret your dreams. The stone of wisdom, jade helps us to reach wise decisions too. Jadeite is the symbol of purity, steadfastness and all things enduring. When struck it gives a musical note, which probably gave rise to the ancient belief that it was a 'charm of harmonious omen'.

YOUR LUCKY NUMBERS

Your lucky numbers are ★ 1 for Taurus ^ & 6 for Venus (also, see 'Lucky Magic Square of Venus')

LUCKY MAGIC SQUARE OF VENUS

In Western occult tradition, each planet has traditionally been associated with a series of numbers and particular arrangements of those numbers. One such method of numerological organisation is the magic square. Magic squares date back to ancient times, appearing in China about 3,000 years ago. The first Chinese square is seen in the scroll of the river Lo - the Lo-Shu, a scroll believed to have been created by Fuh-Hi, the mythical founder of Chinese civilisation. Certain squares came to be linked with the planets; these associations came from the Babylonians. Each *kamea*, or magic square, is linked with a particular planet, and each of the squares has a *seal*, which is the geometric pattern created by following the numbers in order of their value. This pattern touches upon all the numbers of the square and the seal is used to represent the entire square. An intelligence and a spirit are also associated with each kamea, derived from the key numbers contained within it, using a Hebrew form of numerology. This intelligence is viewed as an inspiring, guiding and informing entity.

The 'Magic Square of Venus ' is divided into 49 cells, or squares, seven across and seven down. Each square contains a number between 1 and 49. The sum of the numbers in the vertical, horizontal and diagonal lines is a constant of 175. The total of these numbers is 1225. Therefore, the numbers 7, 49, 175 and 1225 are also assigned to Venus.

YOUR NUMEROLOGY NUMBER & LUCKY SUN SIGN NUMBERS

"Everything that exists has a vibration. The vibration of sound, music, colour, matter, even our words, thoughts, and names show form. All vibration is measurable. To measure we need numbers. Numbers are the basis of all. Numbers are the key to all mysteries."
Shirley Blackwell Lawrence, *Behind Numerology*

Numerology is essentially the metaphysical * 'science' of numbers. The use of numbers in magic is its cornerstone of power. The ancient Greek philosopher and mathematician Pythagoras, born around 590 BC, embarked on a thirty-year spiritual quest studying with important religious and esoteric teachers and healers to find the mystery of 'The Hidden Light', and came to see mankind as living in three worlds: the natural, the human and the Divine. He asserted that all things can be expressed in numerical terms, because they are ultimately reducible to numbers. Pythagoras stated that "Numbers are the first things of all of Nature" and followed the theory that "Nothing can exist without numbers."

Many believe that numbers have an arcane, mystical relationship with words, and with inanimate and animate objects; the interpretations that arose from these relationships date back to a time when the dawning intelligence of primitive man first visualised the meaning of numbers and associated it with spiritual significance. Numerology is the science of the exploration of this relationship in order to discover hidden meanings, forecast the future or interpret the character of a person. In its more modern applications, a series of figures which correspond to an individual's name and date of birth are calculated, and practitioners believe one's prospects, fortune and character can be deciphered from the results ^.

So what is numerology and how does one use it? Everything in the Universe has a vibrational frequency, an energy, a force, all vibrating at various rates, and we as humans are no exception, the difference between one person and another is their rate of vibration. This force or energy is constantly in motion and changing, and we can even 'tune into' and feel our vibrations if we are still for long enough.

Along with letters, sounds, colours, crystals, and many other things, it is believed that numbers also have vibrations, and when we are able to familiarise ourselves with our own numerical frequencies, we can use this familiarity to add power and magic to our lives. The numbers of our birth date, the letters of our names, and the numbers of our Sun sign and ruling planets, all have a unique vibrational frequency, and herein lies the key to understanding our self and our journey through life. Numerology refers to the knowledge contained within the numbers of our birth date and our name, and this is our own personal magic which can greatly assist us through life.

* Metaphysics is the study of those sciences that extend beyond the physical or tangible

HOW TO FIND YOUR NUMEROLOGY NUMBER

^ Your Sun sign's number was added up according to the principle of corresponding a number with a letter, for example 1=A, 2=B, 3=C and so on in sequence and up to 9=I, then beginning again at number 1 for the next letter J and following this same sequence. Following this system, the sum of the letters in Taurus vibrates to the number 1.

Your personal numerology number is determined by adding up all the numbers in your birth date until they reach a two-digit figure. The two resulting numbers are then added together again to form a single digit, which is your personal numerology number. For example, someone born on 3 February 1983, would add the digits $3 + 2 + 1 + 9 + 8 + 3 = 26 =$ (reduced to two digits) 8. So that person's personal numerology birth number is 8.

Each primary number or birth number from 1 to 9 has a specific meaning and is governed by a planetary force. The principle of numerology reduces all numbers down to the following: 1 to 9, and 10, 11, 13 and 22 *. The last four numbers only apply to people specially concerned with the occult and spiritualism - and can be studied at greater length through other sources if so desired - and can in any case be reduced further to a single digit if preferred. Your birth number contains a unique power, and therein lie your strengths, shortcomings and opportunities. It is beyond the scope of this book to outline your individual numerology number possibilities, so for the purposes of astrological applications, I have only included your Sun sign and ruling planet's special numbers.

* The numbers 10 and 13, and the master numbers 11 and 22, can be further reduced to one digit if so desired; however, they can be interpreted as they are without further reduction. The choice is personal.

BASIC MEANINGS & KEYWORDS

1 ★ Sun. Masculine influence, beginnings, independence, inventiveness, originality, leadership, exploration, innovation, ambition

2 ★ Moon. Feminine influence, cooperation, partnership, tact, diplomacy, harmony, unity, emotions, imagination, adaptability

3 ★ Jupiter. Communication, expression, youthfulness, self-confidence, creativity, inspiration, optimism, curiosity

4 ★ Uranus. Order, form, security, stability, patience, restriction, work, values, practicality

5 ★ Mercury. Freedom, inconsistency, change, variety, travel, activity, learned

6 ★ Venus. Love, home, family, sense of duty, responsibility, marriage, justice, nurturing, balance, gentleness, peace, friendship

7 ★ Neptune. Analysis, wisdom, mystical, spiritual, solitude, precision, research, integrity, mystery, psychic perceptions

8 ★ Saturn. Money, power, success, organisation, hard work, business, health, purpose, control, authority, mastery

9 ★ Mars. Completion, endings, Universal, service, humanity, philanthropy, loyalty

10 ★ Fortunate, creative, vibrant, stable, optimistic, original, successful, determined, individualistic

11 ★ Master number. Prophecies, inspiration, moral courage, missionary, long-suffering, foolhardiness, enlightenment, invention

13 ★ Misunderstood, fearful, changeable, interested in the occult, fatalistic, flexible, sacred, beguiling

22 ★ Master number. Powerful, successful, idealistic, attracted to the occult, creative, wise, successful, masterful, spiritually understanding

★ THE NUMBER 6 - FOR VENUS ★

Names ★ Sextile, Hexad, Senary, Sextet, Sextuple, Hexagon

Arithmomantic connections with the letters of the alphabet ★ F, O and X

Ruled by Venus, the number 6 is a loving, stable and harmonious vibration. A perfect number because it is the sum of its factors (1, 2, 3), 6 is balanced, and is associated with family love and domesticity. Number 6 people are very reliable and trustworthy, but may be obstinate. The Hexagon, the number 6 or the Hexad is represented geometrically as a 6-sided, balanced figure. It is also symbolised by two intersecting triangles known as the Seal of Solomon.

Considered a sacred number to some religions who believe that the world was created in 6 days, as such the double triangle was and is frequently carved in stone or painted on windows in old monasteries and churches. In nature we find many examples of the hexagonal in the form of crystals, which are a complete and very comprehensive class in themselves.

On the whole, the Hexas has always been considered one of the happiest numbers, since it represents perfect harmony and completion. As well, 6 has long been regarded as a particularly lucky number, with great balance. It possesses an extremely harmonious nature, associated with love, service and responsibility. Symbolised by the 6-pointed star, its colours are pale blues, turquoises, greens and indigo. It denotes equilibrium, and the six-pointed star is comprised of two triangles, one pointing upwards towards the 'spirit' or heavens, and the other pointing down towards the body or Earth, symbolising balance between them. This association with balance is partly due to the qualities of a cube, a six-sided figure which has shown great stability whichever way up it appears. The cube also displays an equal face in all four directions, plus a face pointing towards the heavens, the so-called fifth or esoteric dimension. Each side of the die is numbered, with six the highest and therefore the most fortuitous of the numbers.

Number 6 promises fame and the gifts of prophesy to its sympathetic and compassionate subjects who may also suffer from anxiety, jealousy or a quick temper. Carrying the vibe of Venus, it is the number of family, comfort, graciousness and beauty but also represents duty and responsibility. People who wish for a steady way of life, and who enjoy being of service to others will particularly benefit. However, there could be a danger that too much is expected by kith and kin which can lead to tension. Yet 6 is the number of the voice, and therefore highly beneficial for anyone interested in a singing career. They can also be over-protective, unwilling to change, anxious, worrisome, suspicious, superficial, possessive, cynical and emotionally unstable. They are responsible, conventional, self-sacrificing, compassionate, protective, loyal, domestic, fair, idealistic with a flair for teaching and healing. The planet Venus governs devotion in love, but number 6 people are more romantic than sensual. Number 6s are born to sing, so a musical path is well suited to these types. You have a great love of beauty, are usually attractive and have a greater ability to make friends than any other number. Despite a loathing of any kind of discord, you can be quite a stubborn fighter. Your luckiest day is Friday.

Alchemy ★ Six is the principle of reconciliation. In alchemy, it represents the union of fire and water, brought into a harmonious relationship. Six is shown as a hexagon, or a six-pointed star made up of two interlaced triangles, which point above and below, symbolising unity between heaven and Earth.

LUCKY 'MAGIC HOURS' OR 'TIME UNITS'

One rule of magic, luck and power, as already outlined elsewhere in this book, can be found within the well-known phrase, "As above, so below." From the most ancient times, the planets were said to rule Earthly destinies and powers. Days of the week were named after the seven planets which were the only ones then known: Sun Day, Moon Day, Mars Day (French: Mardi), Mercury Day (French: Mercredi), Jove Day (French: Jeudi), Venus Day (French: Vendredi) and Saturn Day.

The planetary hours are based on an ancient astrological system, the Chaldean order of the planets. The Chaldean order indicates the relative orbital velocity of the planets, and from a heliocentric (helios = The Sun) perspective, this sequence also indicates the relative distance of the planets from the Sun (the Sun switching places with the Earth in this sequence), and the distance of the Moon from the Earth.

Before an action is taken in daily life, or a transaction undertaken, for instance, it is possible to choose the appropriate day and hour that will provide the greatest chances of success. By studying the planetary hours system, you will discover which actions are propitious to which of the seven planets or 'star-gods' and at what time it would be advisable to undertake them.

The planetary hours system uses this Chaldean order to divide time, and each planetary hour of the planetary day is ruled by a different planet. The order is repeated, starting with the slowest: Saturn - then, Jupiter, Mars, Sun, Venus, Mercury, Moon, then back to Saturn, Jupiter, Mars, etc, ad infinitum. The planet that rules the first hour of the day is also the ruler of that whole day and gives the day its name. So the first hour of Saturday is ruled by Saturn, the first hour of Sunday by the Sun, and so on. It is important, for the purposes of using specific planetary energies for our magic and wishes, to note that planetary hours are not considered the same length as our normal time-keeping slots of sixty minutes. Each day is split into time periods, day time and night time, beginning at around sunrise and sunset respectively. These two time periods are each divided into twelve equal-length hours, which are the planetary hours. So the planetary hours of the day and the planetary hours of the night will be of different lengths, except during the equinoxes when light and darkness are balanced.

In sequence, the Sun, Moon and the five visible planets each exerts its own special influence over a twenty-four-hour period. I like to call your planet's special day and hour the 'Magic Hour'.

Magic rituals to draw luck and love to you should be conducted at astrologically correct times and with the appropriate instruments, tools, cards, herbs, flowers, oils and plants which are linked with the ruling planet. For example, a love ritual, spell or potion demands a concoction of any or all of the above ruled by Venus. Do not underestimate rulerships, for they wield an unseen power that can help make our dreams, big and small, come true.

Further, as specific hours of each day are ruled by certain planets, if you are really serious about attracting some power, luck or magic into your life, it is imperative that you wish, pray or ask at the most opportune times for your Sun sign. There are two methods you can use for fine tuning your magical workings. The first method is to perform your spell, ritual or wishing on the day your Sun sign's ruling planet during the planetary hour that signifies the essence of what you are asking for (e.g. A Taurean who is looking for a career change might perform a career-seeking ritual on a Friday, during a Saturn-ruled planetary hour [Saturn is the planet concerned with careers]. Alternatively, if you wish to summon the power of your Sun sign's own ruling planet, then that same Taurean might perform their career-seeking ritual on a Saturday (ruled by Saturn) during Venus's planetary hour.)

The nature of that which you are asking for, such as love, travel opportunities, money, career guidance, protection or friendship for example, should always be considered when choosing the day or hour during which your magic will be heightened.

The answer to the question why are there seven days in a week, is a very important one to know in unravelling the secret of your Magic Hours. Ancient people recognised the supreme importance of the seven heavenly spheres, which comprised those which could be seen by the naked eye: The Sun, Moon, Mercury, Venus, Mars, Jupiter and Saturn. They then named each of the seven days of the week after one of those spheres and assigned that planetary 'ruler' to one day of the week. As viewed from Earth, these seven spheres appear to move at varying speeds, and the ancients used this factor to arrange them in order of varying speed. If you intend to use your Magic Hours to attract wonderful things, you must memorise that sequence because it is what forms the basis of the whole system.

Whenever you intend to use your Magic Hours or, perhaps more accurately, Magic *Time Units*, it is important to find out the exact time of sunrise for the area in which you live, as sunrise marks the time when your planet's magic is at its most powerful on its specific day. So, at sunrise on Sunday, the Sun rules the hour following the sunrise, the Moon rules the first hour following sunrise on a Monday, and through the week the pattern is repeated, with each day's ruling planet beginning the cycle in that first hour after dawn. It is logical then, that the rest of the planets, in sequence, follow on with one planet per hour for that day thereafter for the rest of the 24-hour cycle, creating a Magic Hour or Time Unit for each planet throughout the day and night, depending on which planet rules that particular day and is therefore the first in line.

If you wish to explore the idea in more depth, it is worth noting first and foremost that each day contains twenty-four hours, but, depending on the season, day and night will be of varying lengths. In summer, daylight is longer than darkness, whereas the reverse applies in winter. During autumn and spring, day and night are usually about equal. Therefore, although a complete day always contains twenty-four hours, there are not always twelve hours between sunrise and sunset and another twelve hours between sundown and the following sunrise. So, depending on the season (and location), a time unit may be shorter than one hour, longer than one hour, or equal to one hour. So whenever you intend to use your Magic Time Units, it is important to find out the exact time of sunrise and sunset for the area in which you live. The next step is to divide the amount of day time (if day when you wish to work your 'magic', otherwise the same following theory applies to night time) into twelve equal sections by calculating the number of hours and minutes between sunrise and sunset and divide by twelve. An example is if the Sun rises at 6.27 a.m. and sets at 5.49 p.m., the amount of time contained in this day is eleven hours and twenty-two minutes. Convert this total into minutes (682) and then divide that figure by twelve (57). Therefore, each of the twelve daylight time units will be 57 minutes on that day.

Although this wonderful method of using astrology is very ancient, it may be completely new to you. You are in for a pleasant surprise though, because if you are willing to delve into a little research and put the system to the test, rich rewards are in store for you!

YOUR LUCKY DAY ★ FRIDAY

Planet ★ Venus
Basic Energy ★ Socialising & Romance
Basic Magic ★ Love, Friendships, Pleasure, Art, Beauty
Element ★ Air
Colour ★ Green
Energy Keywords ★ Affection, Gentleness, Attraction, Diplomacy, Love, Art, Harmony, Appreciation, Sociability, Consideration, Beauty, Construction, Devotion, Cooperation, Femininity, Romance, Flirtiness

Friday is the day of Venus, your planetary ruler. In commonly used calendars, Friday is the sixth day of the week, though in others it is the fifth. The English name is derived from Old English *Frigedaeg*, a result of an old convention associating the goddess Frigg with the goddess Venus, with whom the day is associated. Good Friday, the day before Easter that commemorates the crucifixion of Jesus, Black Friday, referring to several historical disasters that happened on a Friday, Friday the 13th, and Casual Friday, a relaxation of dress codes adopted in some corporations, are some well-known examples with which Venus's day is associated.

Venus is the goddess often associated with love, but she rules over all kinds of partnerships, and harmony, balance, beauty and aesthetics generally. If you wish to change your image or purchase a work of art for your environment, then Venus can help.

In the folk rhyme 'Monday's Child', 'Friday's child is loving and giving'. It is a day of Love, Relationships, Business Partnerships, Marriage, Beauty, Harmony, Balance, Indulgence, Luxury and Pampering, and an opportune time for making wishes or working magic involving love, relationships, beauty, social gatherings, art, style and romance.

VENUS'S MAGIC TIME UNITS
(BASED ON THE PLANETARY HOURS)
FOR EACH DAY OF THE WEEK

SATURDAY ★ Fifth and Twelfth time units after sunrise
SUNDAY ★ Second and Ninth time units after sunrise
MONDAY ★ Sixth time unit after sunrise
TUESDAY ★ Third and Tenth time units after sunrise
WEDNESDAY ★ Seventh time unit after sunrise
THURSDAY ★ Fourth and Eleventh time units after sunrise
FRIDAY ★ First and Eighth time units after sunrise **

Choose the Hour/s of Venus for any transaction, exchange, activity, initiative, venture or wish which involves love, romance, partnerships, business negotiations, pleasure, leisure, good company, style, art, fast cash, friendships, parties, gatherings, marriage harmony and relationships.

** Please note that for the purposes of simplification, the information regarding 'Venus's Magic Time Units' is a very diluted and simplified version of using magical times to your advantage. These hours cover only daylight hours, or the first twelve hours after sunrise, and do not take into account magical times after sunset or throughout the night.

'Hours' is also a deceptive term, as most 'time periods' used in this system are less than an hour, but for the purposes of simplifying the technique, I refer to them as Magic Hours (to keep with the tradition of the term 'planetary hours') rather than magic 'time units', which is what they really are. Should you wish to do further research on your ruling planet's most powerful time units, or require further information about the planet/s from which you are seeking 'energy' from in order to assist your wish-making, other sources may provide you with more comprehensive and detailed information.

A LITTLE NEW MOON / MAGICAL TIME UNIT WISH RITUAL

Step 1 ~ Choose the Magical Hour and/or day that matches your intentions. The first dawn hour of Sunday, ruled by the Sun, is a great time for all-purpose magic, success, joy, abundance, prosperity, bliss, personal power & all-round expansion.

Step 2 ~ Write out a little wish list with the appropriate coloured pen on the colour paper which corresponds to your desire.

Step 3 ~ Choose a small stone of your choosing that is connected to your wish (or a number of stones, that are perhaps linked with your planetary ruler's number, for example 6 for Venus).

Step 4 ~ Find a nice patch of soil in your garden or any special place to you, dig into it, affirm your wish in your mind, place the crystal/s and piece of paper in the hole, then place a plant on top of the crystal/s and wish list.

Step 5 ~ Fill the soil back in over the roots of the plant and feed it with a little water out of a magical vessel (a small genie bottle would be ideal).

Step 6 ~ Thank the Earth, the Universe and the Sun (or whatever planet you are summoning the power from) for bringing forth your desires.

Step 7 ~ Repeat all day long: "Thank You, Thank You, Thank You!"

Step 8 ~ Watch your plant - and your wish - grow bigger and bigger as time goes on!

YOUR LUCKY CHARM/TALISMANS

The following are three 'materials' or talismanic symbols from which to make your lucky charms, and the planetary energy under which to do it, corresponding with your Sun sign:

TAURUS ★ Emerald, Owl, Silver, Venus

"When any star ascends fortunately, take a stone and herb that are under that star, make a ring of the metal that is congruous therewith, and in that fix the stone with the herb under it."
Henry Cornelius Agrippa, *On Occult Philosophy*

Charms, talismans and amulets are among the oldest forms of magic. A charm or talisman is a symbol, often used to communicate a thought, prayer or wish to, or to make a connection with the Divine. It is usually in the form of an object, which has been imbued with mysterious and magical powers. A charm may be as simple as a stone, a flower or a feather, or it might be a parchment bearing writing; the meaning and significance that you attribute to the symbol is what is important. It can be created by yourself (to best effect) or by someone else, and works as a tool to activate our subconscious mind.

You can use general charms such as a cross, or a universally lucky symbol such as a horseshoe, but you will exude and therefore attract more potency and protection if you make and wear the appropriate charms with the matching gemstone, set in the right metal and created under the corresponding planetary influence. While most people wear silver or gold, cheaper tin or copper may be more appropriate and indeed beneficial for your Sun sign. An amulet (for protection) or a talisman or charm (for luck), must also be made, ordered, designed or purchased on the appropriate day of the week for its power to be most effective. Your day, as previously described, is Friday.

You can even go further and create or buy your amulet or charm at one of the hours and/or days when your planet is exerting its most powerful influence. It may sound complicated and requiring of forethought and effort, but if you are going to summon magic and are superstitious enough to truly *believe* that you can do this (and remember pure belief in something is the starting point of all manifestation), you should be scrupulous enough to do it properly. For your planet's day and time, please consult the information under the previous headings 'Your Lucky Day' and 'Venus's Magic Time Units'.

GODS, GODDESSES, ANIMAL TOTEMS & OTHER 'GUIDES'

Gods, goddesses and guides can be summoned to help you live your life to its optimal best. Some are connected with your Sun sign, while others may be of your own personal choosing, ones you may feel particularly drawn towards. Those which align with your ruling planet and your Sun sign, give a good indication of those who will shine a guiding light along your desired path, but you can choose your own too, based upon exploration, observations, research, meditation or simple intuition - I believe choosing your own, based on your inner *knowing* or guidance system, is a very powerful magical tool. However, to get you started, following are some animal spirit guide ideas for your contemplation. Good luck!

YOUR LUCKY ANIMALS & BIRDS

Bull, Cow, Dove, Cat, Sparrow, Goat, Swan, Rabbit, Songbirds, Beaver

"Somewhere beyond the walls of our awareness ... the wilderness side, the hunter side, the seeking side of ourselves is waiting to return."
Laurens van der Post, *The Heart of the Hunter*

"(People) everywhere are being made acutely aware of the fact that something essentially to life and wellbeing is flickering very low in the human species and threatening to go out entirely. This 'something' has to do with such values as love, unselfishness, sincerity, loyalty to one's best friend, honesty, enthusiasm, humility, goodness, happiness ... fun. Practically every animal has these assets in abundance and is eager to share them, given the opportunity and the encouragement."
Jay Allen Boone, *Kinship with All Life*

Some astrological systems, such as Shamanistic * or Native American Astrology, tell us that the Sun sign we were born under has a corresponding animal totem, which informs us about our characteristics and act as a kind of spiritual guide or mentor throughout our life's journey. These totems are described as Solar totems, because many of them share similarities with the Solar system and the sign the Sun was passing through at the time of our birth, and therefore relate to animals and animal behaviours which also correspond to environmental conditions and seasonal changes. These animals encompass many aspects of the Solar system, from seasonal relationships, to creature instincts, to reciprocal links with the planetary vibrations, and 'clans' within nature that you are inherently closely connected with through your date of birth.

Carl Jung, a master of dream analysis and interpretation, proposed that animals symbolise our natural instincts, operating through our dreams. He theorised that certain dream symbols, among them animals, represent core emotions and concepts, archetypes that will hold true for all of us the world over, regardless of so-called 'divisions' such as sex, customs, age or culture. In *Man and His Symbols*, Jung states that primitive societies believed that each person had a bush soul and a human soul. The bush soul incarnates as a tree or animal - a totem - and when the bush soul is harmed or injured, the human soul is considered injured as well.

Some of the most important and powerful spirit guides are those belonging to the animal kingdom. Both in ancient times and in some traditional modern tribal systems, people consult with animals for their wisdom and personal power. Even though most societies today have drifted away from this connection, it has never really left us, and different creatures continue to communicate with us on both the physical and spiritual planes in an attempt to speak to our souls and spirits.

As part of the teaching world, animals can bring us wisdom and survival skills, while others show us how to adapt, transcend or morph. Others still can remind us the importance of play and humour, and guide us around how to overcome life's challenges. Many are known for their loyalty and ability to love unconditionally and without judgement, while some have a grounded and healthy detachment, remaining true to themselves rather than pleasing others, an important lesson in itself. Whatever the qualities of the unique animal guides for your Sun sign, all have some enlightening soul-awakening traits that can teach us much about our own true inner selves. Ultimately, your animal spirit guides, and in particular your Solar totem animal, endow you with qualities that will enhance your life and help to activate your creativity, wisdom and intuition, helping to heal the broken or return the lost pieces of your soul and reconnect you to the natural world.

Your Solar totem animal (listed last on your lucky birds and animals list) is not the same as an animal spirit guide, which is based on metaphysical principles and is also based on your soul's mission in this embodiment - however, you can definitely make your birth Solar totem animal your spiritual guide if you wish, as you may find that its qualities, traits, symbolism and messages strongly reflect and define your own nature - or what you aspire to become, manifest or draw towards you. Your birth totem power animal comes from a place of trust and innocence, and represents the essence of your creative inner child. If you spend some time meditating on your Solar totem animal, asking what lessons it can teach, and reflect deeply on its character, life and habits, you may find it connects with you on a deep spiritual level and you can make the necessary changes to your life to draw in more magic and power.

Overall, if your life is stagnant or in need of healing or an energy boost, you can request your animal spirit or spirits to come and help you change your vibration, awaken your truth and arouse your inner forces. If you are aware of your animal spirit's presence in your life every day, you can use its particular energies to support, guide and teach you. And above all, pay attention to any signs and expressions of its lessons, and remember to thank your chosen animal guide for helping you.

* Shamanism is a traditional spiritual practice of the Native American culture. A shaman, one who practices this age-old art, is an intermediary between the human world and the world of the spirits. He inherits his magical powers at birth, but spends many years as an apprentice, so that he is usually much older in age before he is able to practice and call upon his skills. People ask for a shaman's help when there is a crisis on either a personal or wider spread scale, such as famine, drought, war or illness. The shaman makes contact with the spirits by going into a trance. First, he may perform a series of rituals, which usually include drumming, singing and chanting, and when these have brought on the right conditions, he leaves his body behind to travel to the other world. There he meets with the spirits of his ancestors, who inform him what must be done to relieve the suffering of his people. If the shaman is asked to cure someone of a dis-ease, then the spirits may accompany him to find the correct medicinal herbs or treatments for his patient.

YOUR FEATURE ANIMAL ★ BEAVER

The Beaver's Message ★ Strength of will; persistence will pay off
Brings the totem gift of ★ Endurance, security through abundance, freedom from attachments
Shares the power energies of ★ Resourcefulness, enduring value, inner security, strategy
Brings forth and teaches the magic of ★ Acceptance of change, perseverance, security, cunning

Beaver is the great builder. It teaches us the power of family and home and teaches us to keep ample options open to stay safe and to prosper. "Take charge, adapt and overcome" is the Beaver's motto. Beavers get the job done with characteristic aplomb and maximum efficiency. Strategic and cunning, the mental acuity of the Beaver will ensure it wins in all endeavours, business and combative. Witty but tactless, they can be possessive and over-demanding.

As expert builders, Beavers build their dams extremely strongly and securely. Because of this expertise, the skills of Beavers have been linked to ancient masonry, and often people born under this totem have past lives associated with this magical art. Studying masonry can even uncover deeper, hidden insights about who you are and who you have been.

Transforming the environment, Beavers are master engineers. Their dams consist of wood held together with mud and leaves; streams are even changed into lakes by their dams. When they vacate an area, the dam gradually decomposes, leaving a fertile meadow where the dam lake once was. In this way, and throughout the building and manifesting process, the Beaver shows us the value of strength and resourcefulness, culminating in new promise and fertility. The Beaver also shows us how to work in harmony with the environment.

The Beaver is the symbol of the group mind, the master builder and the great creator. Loyal and enduring but more than a little arrogant at times, it's ultimately their way or the highway. The Beaver's medicine brings you the wisdom of creativity, persistence and using all available resources. It teaches you to seek and use alternative ways of doing things, to achieve through completion, to understand the dynamics of group work, and not to dam the flow of your life's experiences. Without the human ego meddling in their affairs, the Beaver's group mindset strikes a balance between communication and purpose. A team-oriented mind is also essentially close to the spirit of Oneness, reminding us that we all come from the same source and that every individual in the world, is a unique expression of the original creative energy. This signifies that working together and appreciating the resultant coming together of minds, produces a unification that for many creations is far more effective than individual efforts

Adept at teamwork, Beavers work together to construct their homes, and effectively demonstrate that we can create and manifest things most powerfully when we integrate individual talents and skills within the group, to work together to produce a harmonious whole. The Beaver is indeed one of the master creators and constructors of the animal kingdom, and their medicine is of great assistance to those born under this animal. They can teach you how to build intricate structures within your life - both physically, spiritually, mentally and emotionally, using every resource and idea at your disposal. As they create many entrances and exits in their homes, the Beaver teaches the importance of pliability throughout the stages of creation. Often when we wish to manifest something in physical reality, we see and hold a vision of it, without understanding that the creative process doesn't end there - in fact, it begins with the vision, and during the course of bringing it into materialisation, we change and grow, and often changes and improvements are made *while* it is becoming reality. If you push these ideas aside, you may get stuck mid-creation. Instead, it is important to be flexible throughout the process, and to restructure your plan or your creation accordingly.

As the great builder and manifester, the Beaver teaches people born under its power that you have to act on your dreams to bring them alive, and it is now time for action. When the Beaver symbolism appears in our lives, it may even be telling us that we have been neglecting our dreams - or worse, that we have failed to build a doorway for them to enter our lives. Time to start planning and building!

SPIRITUAL KEEPER ★ EAGLE

Your spiritual keeper guides your spiritual growth and brings illumination. Your spiritual keeper is determined by the season in which you were born. Regarded as the 'keepers' or 'caretakers' of the Universe, the four Directions or alignments were also referred to by the Native Americans as the Four Winds because their presence was *felt* rather than seen. The Direction to which your birth time belongs influences the nature of your inner senses. The East Direction's totem is the Eagle. The Eagle is a symbol of freedom, victory and spirit. It flies higher than any other bird, high enough to 'touch the Sun'. The golden Eagle is a symbol of peace, and an Eagle flying overhead is a sign of Shaman power, sometimes taken as a call to that vocation. To the shaman, the Eagle is a messenger, bringing instructions from the spirit of the night. As Halifax states, "When shamans get power, it always comes from the night." The Eagle is the sacred messenger, flying high to carry our prayers to the Great Spirit and returning with gifts of illumination and clear vision. The Eagle enables us to see the bigger picture, to rise above our Earthly concerns, and reminds us to pay attention to the things that really matter in life. This majestic bird brings you the totem gift of freedom, mission and perfect timing, sharing the power energies and magic of pride, spirit and manifestation. Your animal keeper the Eagle is, above all, a potent symbol of vision and strength.

CLAN ★TURTLE

Your clan animal comes from a place of inner knowing and intuition, helping you to discover the essence and magic of your true self. The Turtle is the totem of the Earth clan and in mythology, during a time when there was only water and nowhere for the people and animals to go, the Turtle made a great sacrifice by letting everyone come and live on her back. In the Far East a talisman carved in the form of a Turtle is believed to have power over all kinds of magic; the Chinese and Japanese also wear charms in the shape of Turtles to ensure a long life. In ancient times, the shape of a Turtle's shell suggested the dome of the sky and the creature became a symbol of heavenly virtue. The medicine of the Turtle is Mother Earth. The Turtle can be your guide to connect with our Earth Mother for healing and wisdom, and reminds us, in return, to tread gently and with respect. In fact, you have a responsibility to our Mother to protect her, and also to remind others to appreciate her bountiful beauty that provides so much for life itself.

People of this clan tend to be brave, stubborn, strong and loyal. Methodical and practical, you possess a great determination but also like to take things one step at a time - with steady, slow-paced grace. Although some Turtle clan people tend to be as hard as a rock, you have a need to personify roots, growth and stability, much like the Earth itself does. You are revitalised most strongly by visiting natural places frequently and instinctively feel connected to rocks; in fact, you instinctively feel drawn to be around rock formations and need to have rocks in some form or another around you in your personal environment. Indeed, the rocks will speak to you, if you listen, but you must be careful not to become too much like them - that is, immovable, inflexible and too firmly rooted in the one place out of a need for comfort, safety or security.

In essence, Turtle clan souls focus on the tasks at hand with the determination, persistence, diligence and perseverance of one who is aligned with a true Mission. To connect with your clan animal, visualise yourself walking at a slow and steady pace, with no worry for shelter as you carry your home on your back. You also have no concern for how fast you are travelling along the Path, for you know that you will arrive exactly where and when you are meant to. Nor do you fear attack from predators as you feel assured that the armour on your back will guard against attack. These lessons, once learned and incorporated into your life, are the blessings of being born of the Turtle.

YOUR CORRESPONDING CHINESE ASTROLOGY ANIMAL

The Chinese Zodiac, known as Sheng Xiao (literally meaning 'birth likeness'), is based on a twelve-year cycle, each year in that cycle related to a particular animal. These animals are: Rat, Ox, Tiger, Rabbit, Dragon, Snake, Horse, Sheep, Monkey, Rooster, Dog and Pig. The selection and order of the animals that so influence people's lives, particularly in East Asian cultures, originated in the Han Dynasty (202 BC - 220 AD) and was based upon each animal's traits, characteristics, tendencies and living habits. Further, ancient people observed that there were twelve Full Moons in a year, and that, among other similarly related celestial observations, suggests its origins are also based on astronomical concepts.

The legend of the Chinese zodiac's story usually begins with the Jade Emperor, or Buddha (depending on who is telling the tale), summoning all the animals of the Universe for a race or a banquet. The twelve animals of the zodiac all appeared at the palace, and the order in which they arrived determined the order of the Chinese zodiac.

Each oriental animal corresponds with a Western astrology sign. For Taurus, it is the Snake.

> "Mine is the wisdom of the ages.
> I hold the key to the mysteries of life.
> Casting my seeds on fertile ground.
> I nurture them with constancy and purpose.
> My sights are fixed.
> My gaze unchanging.
> Unyielding, inexorable and deep
> I advance with steady, unslackened gait,
> The solid Earth beneath me.
> *I am the Snake."*
> **Theodora Lau**

Chinese name for the Snake ★ SHE
Ranking Order ★ Sixth
Hours ruled by the Snake ★ 9 a.m. to 11 a.m.
Direction ★ South - Southeast
Season and principle month ★ Spring - May
Corresponds to the Western sign ★ Taurus

★ **SNAKE** ★ Fixed Element Fire

★ Keywords ★

Quiet, wise, deep-thinking, intuitive, vain, stingy, calm exterior, intense, passionate, regulated, shrewd

The Snake is the sixth animal of the Chinese horoscope. Like Dragons, Snakes don't always have a good image in the West, but they are revered in the East and associated with wisdom. Traditionally a yin sign, Snakes are cultured, wise, sophisticated, intuitive and enjoy the finer things in life. Snakes are elegant and often beautiful, with a certain way about them that makes people look twice. Possessing sensuality and a natural talent for dressing well which add to your allure, you are at your best when asked for advice - and then your wisdom truly shines through. As an intuitive thinker, you will ponder things deeply and quite likely get a good sense of the underlying issues of any matter. As a connoisseur and extravagant spender, you love luxury and style, but you have a certain naivety which belies your worldly appearance. Your charm is highly seductive, but you may be prone to indolence and possessiveness of people and 'things'.

YOUR METALS

Taurean power metals are Copper, Brass and Bronze.

Although the magic power of crystals is widely recognised and applied, the influence radiating from metals is often overlooked. Metal, too, emits a powerful energy and in fact, in Chinese philosophy, metal is considered so essential and powerful that it is classified as one of the elements, alongside Air, Fire, Earth and Water.

As already mentioned earlier in the book, throughout the writings of early philosophers and theorists, there are countless references to the unmistakable mystic connection between the seven known planets of the time, and Earthly affairs, ailments and objects. Seven metals were connected with the seven planets, to which seven colours and the seven 'transformations' were added. So the ancient alchemist came to share the astrological doctrine that each planet ruled a mineral: The Sun ruled gold, the Moon silver, Mars iron, Venus copper, Saturn lead, Jupiter tin, and Mercury quicksilver. Consequently, in alchemical symbolism the same sign came to represent the nominated metal and its corresponding planet.

COPPER

Copper is a chemical element with symbol Cu (from Latin *cuprum*), and carries a special cultural significance in that it was the first metal to be used by humans, its use believed to be as early as 7000 BC. Indeed, there is evidence it has been in use for at least 10,000 years. In alchemy, the symbol for copper was also the symbol for the goddess and planet Venus, your ruler. Aphrodite (Venus's Greek counterpart) and Venus represented copper in alchemy and mythology because of copper's lustrous beauty, its ancient use in producing mirrors, and its association with Cyprus, a place which had sacred links with the goddess.

Copper is a purely positive metal and when worn it is said to attract love (combining copper with emeralds makes a highly successful - and attractive - love amulet). Considered to hold sacred properties by various cultures in North America and India, copper is believed to stimulate healing and romance. Its healing reputation is well-known and widespread in the form of copper jewellery, worn to relieve certain physical ailments, and copper jewellery is also metaphysically used as a talisman to magnetise and maintain love, health, luck and prosperity.

Copper is prized by craftsmen for its elegance and lustre, and its ease of use in crafting things of great aesthetic appeal. For this, it is naturally considered a Venusian metal and so is associated with Taurus and Libra. Pure copper is reddish-orange/gold in colour and is soft and malleable, and like aluminium, it is 100 % recyclable without any loss of quality. As one of only two coloured metals, its attractiveness makes it highly desirable for making ornaments and jewellery.

Copper's main modern-day applications are its use in electrical implements and electrical wires (having very high thermal and electrical conductivity, and being ductile enough to be drawn into wire or beaten into sheets without fracturing), roofing and plumbing, industrial machinery, scientific instruments, and of course coins. The high resonance of copper makes it suitable for use in stringed musical instruments, such as violins, guitars and the double bass (traditional astrological thought associates the art of music with Venus). It is usually used as a pure metal, but when a greater hardness is required, it can be combined with other elements to make an alloy, such as brass or bronze. Copper's resistance to corrosion also makes it suitable for use in, or near the ocean. Brass, an alloy of zinc and copper, is used extensively in marine applications due to its non-corrosive nature.

Copper is even found in the human body in trace amounts and has various biological functions, mainly in the liver, muscle and bone.

Copper can also be made into jewellery, and it is believed that wearing a copper bracelet can relieve arthritis-related symptoms *^. It is also used in alternative medicine to various other ailments, as its absorption through the skin somehow creates a magnetic field, thereby affecting or treating nearby tissues ^.

Overall, copper serves many purposes and is arguably essential in keeping the world functioning, as it pervades in all facets of (comfortable) existence: it is found in your house, coin currency, transport systems, computers, cars, and cruise ships - all pretty essential things for the true Venusian experience, don't you think?

* However, in various studies, no difference has been found between arthritis treated with a copper bracelet, magnetic bracelet or placebo bracelet
^ Please check with a medical professional before applying any remedy, treatment or concept outlined here.

PLANTS, HERBS, SPICES, TREES, SHRUBS, FLOWERS, SCENTS & INCENSE

Plants have long been associated with magic, medicinal properties, superstition, nutrition and even astrology. In ancient times, some were endowed with magical properties based upon beliefs of the time, but also upon anecdotal evidence that some herbal concoctions, flowers or essences helped alleviate and even cure uncomfortable, painful or dis-eased physical or mental states. Whether these were based upon 'old wives' tales' or beliefs in supernatural forces matters little, for in modern times we can prove and indeed *have* proven through scientific research and controlled experiments, that plants have their place in our health and medicine cabinets. Some 'magical' plants have aphrodisiac or narcotic properties, while others have formidable toxic effects, but all are considered in some way to affect the human system on physical, spiritual and psychological levels. Plants such as cocoa, tobacco and coffee, which have accompanied humans over the course of millennia, are still, more than ever, an integral part of our daily lives. They still incite the same pleasures, the same fascinations, and the same dangers, and some still carry the same taboos. It is interesting to note that more than 80 per cent of chemical medicines in existence today, and found in pharmacists' dispensaries, are made from plants.

In modern astrology herbs are often associated with the zodiac signs and have evolved from an old system where a specific planet rules each herb. The planet that governs a herb is chosen according to its appearance, scent and where it grows; herbs are additionally categorised as hot or cold, and dry or moist. In this way you can see how the nature of the herb corresponds to the nature of the planet. If you are familiar with your ruling planets' basic associations, you will find it easy to match it to herbs. Although you can simply buy whatever herbs you wish to use for your magic, the optimum effect will be obtained if you can gather them at a favourable astrological time. Once you are armed with astrological knowledge, you can choose a time when the planet that rules your chosen herb is in a position of strength. Keep in mind that each planet rules a substantial amount of plants, so if one isn't easily obtained, it should be simply to find another one to use for the same purpose.

There sometimes seems to be a wide variance in the list of herbs associated with a specific astrological influence. This is because the different parts of the plant have different rulerships and uses. For example, whichever planet rules it, a plant that bears fruit is naturally related to Jupiter, its flowers relate to Venus, seed or bark to Mercury, leaves to the Moon, wood to Mars, and roots to Saturn. So, as well as the planet that traditionally rules the plant, it can be regarded as having a secondary ruler according to the part of the plant being used. Although you don't need to work with a highly complex system of deciding which herb will suit your purposes, you can make your magical workings more powerful by paying attention to some of these nuances.

Essentially, different scents, herbs, flowers and plants have their own specific vibrations. Their essences should be worn on your skin (you can make up your own combinations using essential oils or flower waters), burned in an oil burner, inhaled from a cloth, diffused in a bath or bowl of steam, or burned as incense sticks. Many plants, herbs and spices, however used, contain gentle yet effective energies which will affect not only your wishing ceremonies, but also your moods, associations and emotions, which can assist in carrying your wonderful Self in the direction of your dreams. Lifted up on incense smoke, for example, your wish is carried out to the wider Universe. Try making your own, out of any or all of your power plants, woods, flowers, shrubs, trees or herbs!

Thirty-three magical, mythical plants are: Cocoa, rosemary, tobacco, thyme, wheat, coffee, sugar cane, cinnamon, hemp, tea, pumpkin, foxglove, incense, amanita (a mushroom), tarragon, pepper, rice, belladonna, reed, ginseng, clove, ginger, sage, maize, mistletoe, lily, mandrake, St John's Wort, poppy, peyote, cinchona, verbena and the vine *. How many of your Taurean 'lucky plants' (listed under the next sub-category, 'Your Lucky Plants, Herbs, Spices', etc.) can be found on this Magical 33 List?

YOUR LUCKY PLANTS, HERBS, SPICES, TREES, SHRUBS, FLOWERS, SCENTS, OILS & INCENSE

Rose, Poppy, Lily, Spearmint, Goldenrod, Sorrel, Gentian, Wheat, Sweet Pea, Crab Apple, Dog Rose, Artichokes, Silverweed, Daffodil, Liquorice, Coltsfoot, Bearberry, Garden Mint, White or Purple Lilac, Larkspur, Bearberry, Lovage, Peach, Pear, Slippery Elm, Violet, Foxglove, Moss, Vine, Dandelion, Daisy, Narcissus, Flax, Sage, Walnut, Lavender, Tansy, Sycamore, Fig, Lily of the Valley, Olive, Thyme, Almond, Plum, Lemon Verbena, Ash, Carnation, Cypress, Apple, Myrtle, Parsley, Coriander, Cloves, Oregano, Peppermint, Lovage Root, Vervain, Chamomile, Fenugreek, Primula, Violet, Columbine. *

For Venus ★ Coriander, Valerian, Thyme, Myrtle. Venus is the planet of beauty, and the plants related to it contain fruits and a pleasant fragrance. Blackberry, Wild Cherry, Motherwort & Raspberry are all connected with Venus *

* Some plant products can be poisonous, toxic, hallucinogenic or even fatal if consumed. Always research first.

YOUR SPECIAL POWER FLOWERS

TAURUS IN GENERAL ★ Poppy

OTHER BIRTH FLOWERS ★ Foxglove, Rose, Primula, Violet, Daisy & Columbine

APRIL BORN ★ Sweet Pea ★ Together with grace and a sense of delicacy, the sweet pea brings with it the possibility of a varied life for the versatile April-born.

MAY BORN ★ Lily of the Valley ★ Lily of the Valley is a very auspicious birth flower, symbolising joy, optimism, and bright, new beginnings throughout life. Lily of the Valley signals the return of happiness.

YOUR FOODS

"If alcohol is added, the Taurean can closely resemble King Henry VIII, happily gorging at a royal banquet."
Linda Goodman

Home and hearth, meadow and hayloft live at the sensual heart of Taurus appetites. Warm them, sweeten them and always replace novelty with solidity. Stable, consistent, affectionate and loving, the Taurean is a bit of a connoisseur when it comes to food and there is very little that will turn your appetite off. Dense meats are favourites, and you will almost always go back for seconds and relish any leftovers. You love most cuisines, as all types of foods appeal to you, however you are not adventurous and are shy when trying new things; you would prefer to stick with the tried, tested and true.

An easy going and predictable routine is best suited to you, as you don't like eating at strange hours or on the run. Your ruling planet Venus rules the colour green, and earthy, leafy produce is a must in your kitchen. Loving of comfort and luxury, you enjoy robust, hearty, sustaining pleasures of the plate and palate - and no expense will be spared. Being ruled by your physical senses, you don't just eat with your eyes first, but rather *all* your faculties, before the food even hits your tastebuds. Aromatic food appeals to your senses, as does lavish presentation. You adore dining out in expensive restaurants, being waited on by your loved one, and equally love waiting on others, as you make both an excellent cook and a delightful host. Overall, the more tender loving care, time and patience are put into making the dish, the more appealing you will find it! Slow-cooked and home-style were made for the Taurean palate. Fast, poorly presented, exotic and adventurous are definitely not on the menu for the Bull.

TAURUS POWER FOODS

"Let food be your medicine; let medicine be your food."
Hippocrates

Taurean power foods are piquant, perfumed, aromatic and dense. Soft Fruits (Currants, Berries, Pears, Mangoes, Raisins, Apricots, Bananas, Guavas, Lychees, Peaches), White Meats and Seafood Served With Fragrant Marinades, Breads, Wheat and Oat-Based Foods, Zucchinis, Green Capsicum, Sweet Corn, Cabbage, Artichokes, Grapes, Beans, Peas, Asparagus, Spinach, Apples, Carrots, Plantains, Beetroot, Cereals and Ginger are also appealing to the Taurean palate. Your power beverages are Rich Earthy Coffee, Expensive Wines, Rich Liqueurs, Whisky, Rum and Rye. *

* Caution: Always use essential oils, alcohol and/or herbs with caution and research each one prior to use, as not all are safe for use by certain people, or under certain conditions such as pregnancy, intoxication or illness. Some herbs and oils may be hallucinogenic, toxic in high doses, or produce other undesirable effects, and may be considered potentially harmful or hazardous if used or consumed before operating machinery, driving, or combined with alcohol or other drugs. Always consult a qualified practitioner or undertake thorough research from reliable sources before use or consumption of any of the listed essential oils, herbs or foods.

YOUR LUCKY WOOD ★ SYCAMORE
(Great to make a magic wand out of!)

Native Americans referred to trees as 'Standing People' because they stand firm, obtaining strength from their connection with the Earth. They therefore teach us the importance of being grounded, while at the same time listening to, and reaching towards, our higher aspirations. In Norse mythology, Yggdrasil, the tree of life, is a cosmic map that represents all life. The tree has its roots in the Underworld, is linked to the Earth through its trunk and its branches reach into the air of the Otherworld of spirit. The dryad, or tree's spirit, needs to be respected and asked when 'taking' from a tree for the purposes of magic.

The essence of tree magic lies in understanding the qualities of each type. These can be drawn on for such things as healing and spell-casting. For example, the rowan tree grows high up the sides of mountains, often in hard-to-reach places, so if you need to develop tenacity or access to difficult spiritual spaces, you can call on this tree; the oak tree is durable and strong, so if you are needing fortification or firmness, you can gain power from this tree. When respected as living, breathing beings, trees can provide insights into the workings of Nature, cycles, and our own inner essence. Each birth time is associated with a particular kind of tree, the basic qualities of which complement the nature of those born during that time. Appreciate the beauty of your affinity tree and study its nature carefully, for it has a connection with your own nature and lessons to impart.

SYCAMORE ★ Bestowing gifts of divination, prosperity, strength, love and harmony, sycamores are one of the oldest tree species on Earth. Symbolising growth, versatility, persistence and endurance, the sycamore is water-resistant and often grows where other trees cannot. In magic, it is useful for askings involving growth, and having regenerative properties, can be used for restorative purposes. Sycamore symbolises development, vitality and perseverance and is good to use for any magic involving prosperity, love and longevity. Believed to bring success and abundance, it can also teach humility.

YOUR SACRED CELTIC CALENDAR TREES
★ WILLOW OR HAWTHORN

WILLOW ★ (15 April - 12 May)
HAWTHORN ★ (13 May - 9 June)

The Celts and other ancient peoples had many beliefs and traditions based around the magical lore of trees. The system of Celtic tree astrology was developed out of a natural connection with the Druids' knowledge of Earth cycles and their reverence for the sacred knowledge they believed was held by trees. The Druids had a profound connection with trees and regarded them as vessels of infinite wisdom. Their calendar, being based on a Lunar year of thirteen months, contains a tree for each of these

Lunar months, corresponding with (but not exactly) each of the twelve western astrology zodiac signs, which are based on the Solar calendar. Because there are some crossovers, I have included two possible trees for your zodiacal birth period.

WILLOW ★ Willow is traditionally found on riverbanks, growing its roots in water, connecting it with the influence of the Moon. The willow symbolises regeneration as cut willows always re-sprout. It is a fast-growing, hardy and resilient tree, being able to withstand severe frosts. With more than 300 evolving variants, the willow is a powerful survivor and revered symbol of witchcraft and enchantment. The wood of willow is tough but elastic, and so highly flexible that it has traditionally been used for the making of baskets. In fact, it was an important resource for ancient communities, providing withies for wicker baskets - 'Witch', 'Wicca' and 'wicked' are said to be derived from the word wicker. As a water-dwelling tree, it signifies emotional balance, intuition and water-divining magic.

Willow is the tree of emotion, love, intuition and poetic inspiration. Ruled by Cerridwen, Celtic Moon goddess worshipped by the Welsh, a deeply mysterious figure, who is the keeper of the flaming cauldron of Divine wisdom, where immortal knowledge and the fires of inspiration are formed, the willow can gently guide us towards this illumination. Because of its connection with the Lunar sphere, its powers are said to be most effective when used at night, under the Moon. Willow types are in tune with the mystical aspects of the Moon, making them highly creative, intuitive and perceptive.

HAWTHORN ★ With its white flowers (virginal), red berries (fertility) and sharp thorns (maturity), the hawthorn tree symbolises the three aspects of the Mother Goddess: those of maiden, mother and crone. It is suitable for use by those interested in exploring the Female Mysteries.

Throughout western Europe, the hawthorn is greatly esteemed as a magical tree bearing protective and visionary powers in addition to its renown amongst herbalists as a heart-healer. The haw in the word means 'hedge', as the thorny-branched trees, which attain a height of up to thirty feet, were planted as hedgerows to separate fields and prevent grazing animals from passing into a neighbour's meadow by virtue of the tree's inch-long thorns. In the European autumn time, the creamy hawthorn blossoms transform into clusters of ruby-red berries and the waxy leaves turn crimson.

Hawthorn has a magical reputation and association with being a portal into 'other worlds'. In Celtic tradition, it was believed that a hawthorn tree found growing with oak and ash was a sacred place in which fairies dwelled, and that if one slept under the hawthorn at Full Moon in May or on May Eve, that one would behold entrance into the land of the sprites. It certainly couldn't hurt to try

The wood of the hawthorn is fine-grained and therefore suitable for carving delicate items and magical objects. Some traditions even believe hawthorn can carry our wishes into the ether. In times past, travellers hung bits of ribbon on the thorns of this holy tree, murmuring wishes into the cloth. When moved by the wind, these strips whisper the wishes into the ears of fairies who whimsically bestow gifts upon humans. And like many relatives of the rose tree, hawthorn can also be used in love spells to attract one's true love. As the guardian of the doorway to fairy realms, hawthorn wisely discerns the right timing for a wounded heart to open. Hawthorn berries and blossoms can be used to ease the grief of a broken heart and also to open it up to new love.

Hawthorn types are the grand illusionists of the Celtic tree system. You are not what you appear to be. Your outward persona is different to your inner self. While appearing to live a seemingly average life, inside you are burning with the passion of an inexhaustible creative flame. Versatile and well-adjusted, you can adapt to most life situations easily. With a healthy sense of humour and a clear understanding of irony, you are naturally curious and have a broad interest in a wide variety of topics. Possessing amazing insights and the ability to see the bigger picture, you often under-credit yourself for your astute observations.

ESPECIALLY FOR AUSTRALIANS
(OF ALL ZODIAC SIGNS)

If you live in Australia, here are two Australian-based magical woods, for those who prefer to source their woods closer to home and nature. Australia has a less documented history than many European civilisations, but still has no less mythology and legends swirling in its mists of time.

EUCALYPTUS ★ Eucalyptus is very plentiful and has a wonderfully intoxicating, distinctive, clean aroma which is reminiscent of the continent's vast areas of bushland, and has played an important ceremonial and medicinal role in the culture of Australian Aborigines, who have inhabited the nation for 40,000 to 50,000 years. Eucalyptus is a wood of feminine energy whose elemental association is Earth and main origin is Australia. One of the strongest healing woods known, eucalyptus wood has been used for centuries for medicinal as well as ritualistic purposes. Heady and Earthy, the energy of this wood is clean and pure. Eucalyptus is recommended for the promotion of good, robust health, and is also related to luck, especially if regarding knowledge. An excellent tool in divination, particularly when worn as a charm to invoke luck, it brings the wearer or user good fortune when used in rituals seeking positive results.

LEOPARDWOOD (or LACEWOOD) ★ Leopardwood or the Leopard Tree, so named because of its spotted wood, carries the energies of both the masculine and the feminine, Mars (Aries, Scorpio) and Venus (Taurus, Libra), and its main affinity is with the Water element (Cancer, Scorpio, Pisces). Leopardwood is a very useful tool for divination and is associated with positive luck, earning it the label 'gambler's wood'. Overall, its energy is very positive, making it an ideal wood for use in almost any ritual or spell, especially those concerning luck, magic and divination.

THE POWER OF LOVE

Each Sun sign exudes their own love and romance style. This style is an energy unique to that sign, and has the power to magnetise to that person their true, soulful match. Unhappy or unsuccessful relationships are often the result of incompatible Sun signs, personal values, goals, hopes, viewpoints or expectations. I believe everyone has a perfect soul partner (or three!) who is especially for them, and just knowing that special person or persons are out there can illuminate your life's romantic path. In this lifetime, we may not find that person or persons, but can still experience the joys and wonders of many other significant relationships which enrich and add tremendous meaning to our lives. Some partnerships are only fleeting, but the feelings they give us can last a lifetime, while others are more enduring, and the rewards they give us and lessons they teach us can last a lifetime too. Small gestures of love on a frequent basis, consistent nurturing and communication, and making the effort to understand each other, are just four ways to keep the fires of passion and romance burning long after the initially roaring fire has diminished into glowing embers.

Your whole natal chart would need to be examined to form an overall picture of your romantic nature, and although the Sun is a fantastic starting point, it is not the sole consideration. Regarding these other planets, in Carl Jung's studies on psychological astrology, and in traditional synastry (the comparing of two people's natal charts to determine overall compatibility), the harmonious link between the Sun in one person's chart and the Moon in the other's (usually the man's Sun and the woman's Moon) is considered the best indication for a happy and enduring relationship. More specifically, the sextile aspect, an angle of 60 degrees, appeared most frequently between the Sun of one and the Moon of the other in fulfilling relationships. Other positive planetary contacts, such as one person's Moon to another's Venus, or the Mars to the Moon (again, traditional indications of attraction and harmony) also occurred frequently.

The feminine personal planets in a male's chart (Moon and Venus), and the masculine personal planets in a female's chart (Sun and Mars) tell a lot about the inner self and how this is projected onto relationships. However helpful chart analysis is in telling a story about your relationship style and approach, it all depends not on your chart, but on what you do with the resources at your disposal, which your chart can indeed tell you a lot about. Relationships and marriages involving harmonious planetary and zodiacal energies between the two people tend to last longer because they are simply more 'flowing' and easier.

The signs in which the four personal and 'relationship' planets - the Sun, the Moon, Venus and Mars - are placed, coupled with the aspects they make with the other planets in the chart, give important clues into understanding the often unconscious drives within you that shape your relating style, tastes, mannerisms and patterns.

Expanding upon the other planetary considerations is beyond the scope of this book, but it is useful to know, particularly if you are interested in examining the dynamics of a current relationship a bit deeper, or are wishing to attract a new one into your life. But for now, your Sun sign is a wonderful place to start! Your Solar sign is regarded as being at the core of the complex - and very fun - study of relationships! So for now, we will begin this study of love with your essence, your core self, the brightest light shining from within - your Sun sign!

SOME LUCKY-IN-LOVE TIPS
GENERAL HINTS

★ To attract and retain love, the Heart chakra (an energy centre within the body) needs to be balanced and clear from blockages. The Heart chakra is located in the region of the physical heart. Its Sanskrit name is *anahata*, and its symbol is a twelve-petal green lotus flower whose centre contains a green circle and two intersecting triangles making up a six-pointed star representing balance (and also could be said to symbolise six as the number of Venus). Its element is Air and its colour is green. Balance in this chakra is expressed as unconditional love for ourselves and others. Crystals that can be used to cleanse and balance this chakra are mostly green and pink stones.

★ Pink candles (two, representing a couple, or six, representing Venus, is preferable) can be used in love spells.

★ Any 'love-attracting' wishing rituals should be done on a Friday (ruled by Venus) night around the time of the New Moon (signifying the principle of increase and growth).

★ Basil, otherwise known as witch's herb or St Joseph's wort, is said to be the most potent lover herb of all. Basil vibrates to the energy of Mars, which is all about lust and sexual energy, and it is used prolifically in all sorts of love potions and rituals throughout the world.

★ Ginger has a reputation as a potent sexual tonic and aphrodisiac *. Arousing and warm, it can increase sensual vitality, particularly in men. Being warming and spicy, its vibration aligns with Mars. Saffron is also regarded as a potent, albeit expensive, aphrodisiac!

★ Wear red and pink (associated with Mars and Venus respectively), as these colours in all their shades are said to incite passion, lust and romance. Green is also connected with the heart by virtue of its association with the Heart chakra and the planet Venus, and its links with fertility, nature, abundance of all kinds, and new growth.

★ Call upon some higher spiritual help. When working your 'love magic', some planetary influences, goddesses and gods that you can call upon are: Aphrodite, Venus and Eros/Cupid, and other lesser known deities such as Juno Lucina, Demeter, Freya, Ishtar, Circe and Hathor.

★ The planet Venus has developed a rich culture of gods and goddesses associated with her varying levels of love and passion. These include the virgin - Brighid; the fertile woman - Aphrodite, (the Greek goddess); and of course Venus (the Roman equivalent); the mother and provider - Demeter; and desirous or physical love - Eros/Cupid (Venus's son).

★ The pine tree is sacred to Adonis (Venus's lover) and is said to balance the male and female energies. Pine is cleansing and protective and, as an evergreen, symbolises life. Its cones represent fertility.

★ Cardamom is said to have aphrodisiac qualities.

★ The three almost universally recognised symbols of love are the goddesses Venus and Aphrodite, and the Cupid. Venus is the patroness of flowers and vegetation, and represents the regenerative cycle of creation, as well as beauty, herbs and physical love. She can be called upon for general love wishes and rituals. The dove, roses, rings, copper, apples, rosemary and the ankh are some of her sacred symbols. Aphrodite is a Greek goddess who has the ability to brings lovers together. Her name means 'of the sea' as she is believed to have been born of the foam of the ocean. She can be called upon in ceremonies and spells for affection, love, marriage and partnership. Some of her associated symbols are the Flower of Aphrodite, swans, dolphins, frankincense and myrrh. Cupid, the cherubic winged boy with a bow and arrow, is the Roman name, and Eros is the Greek name for the same deity. The son of Venus/Aphrodite, he is an aspect that represents lustful love and desire.

★ Heartsease, another name for the wild pansy, Latin viola tricolour, was one of the most popular additives to the love potions of the ancient Romans and Greeks.

★ In centuries past, when people were more in tune with nature and its cycles, ceremonies, rituals and festivals were held on certain dates or times of year. The following are some examples, and you can reawaken their powers through craft and ceremony: February 2 is Bridhid's Day, or Bride's Day, and represents the white goddess; February 14 is Valentine's Day, traditionally the greatest and most well-known love 'celebration' of the year; March 1 is one of the festival days of Juno Lucina, the light bearer and goddess of women and marriage; the month of April is especially linked to the love goddess Aphrodite; the Summer solstice which falls on or around June 21 is an important time for reconnecting with the spirit of love, fertility and marriage; August 1 is the first of three harvest festivals in the Celtic calendar: The Harvest Festival honours Demeter, the goddess of love, as bountiful mother and faithful wife; the Festival of Lights, Diwali, in October, is sacred to Lakshmi, the Hindu goddess of happiness, love, and good fortune; the Winter solstice which falls on or around December 21, marks the turning point from long dark nights to lengthening days, and is the time of the wheel of love when virgin goddesses gave birth to their children - it is also fittingly symbolised by evergreens such as pine, ivy and holly; in Mexico, December 31, the last night of the year, is traditionally 'wishing night' and is an opportune time to make a wish for a lover in the coming year, using evergreen branches to enhance your request.

* The term 'aphrodisiac' is derived from Aphrodite, the Greek goddess of love, beauty, lust and sensuality

★ GEMSTONES ★

When it comes to calling love into your life using crystals, the general rule is that any of the pink or green stones are closely aligned with matters of the heart and can therefore help you to entice the affections you seek. Although your Sun sign has its very own special gemstones, outlined elsewhere in the book, the following stones can be used by all the signs (except for the first point, which are your own sign's feature stones), as their energies and qualities contain the power to attract and create love in all its forms, from self-love to deeper soulful connections with another, or to increase states of being which open the heart, thus enhancing your abilities to magnetise love.

★ Emerald, Sapphire and Diamond. Using your Taurean luckiest crystals is a fabulous start to working on heightening your romantic zest, and making your sensual energy more potent. Jade and Rose Quartz are also useful in raising your attracting powers.

★ Rose Quartz is the ultimate love stone. It invites love into your life by helping to open your heart to receive love, and gently reminding you that you are worthy of love. Connected with the Heart chakra, it is the stone of unconditional love, enhancing all forms of it and opening up the heart. It is excellent for increasing self-worth and acceptance. The colour of rose quartz is pink, the colour of Venus, the amorous planet of desire and nurturance. Balancing and calming, it helps to heal emotional pain. Wear this stone, keep some beside your bed, or sleep with some under your pillow to remind you that love it coming your way - and that you whole*heart*edly deserve it!

★ Green Aventurine is considered the 'opportunity and luck stone'. Connected with the Heart chakra, it helps us to recognise opportunities and is said to place us exactly where we need to be for good things to transpire, as energetically it opens our mind and heart to increased perception to recognise lucky elements. It also promotes new growth, optimism, and is an overall attractor of good fortune, adventure and abundance.

★ Jade, on a spiritual level, has an affinity with the Heart chakra. It harmonises relationships, and encourages compassion and the establishment of strong bonds.

★ Emerald is reputedly a stone of constancy in love, and is said to have been brought to Earth from the planet Venus. Because it is green, it also holds deep associations with the Heart chakra.

★ Rhodochrosite can be used to attract one's soul mate. This stone, as with all the pink stones, can be used as an effective love magnet. It encourages you to appreciate yourself by teaching you that you are worthy of love, wholeness and happiness - and so opening you up to receive.

★ Malachite, Citrine, Rhodonite, Moonstone, Morganite, Beryl, Ruby, Mangano Calcite, Garnet, Red and Pink Tourmaline, Tugtupite, Rutilated Quartz, Lodestone, Peridot and Lapis Lazuli are also known for their love properties, and can be used or worn to invite romance into your life, or to bring and retain enduring love.

★ Clear Quartz can be used with any of these listed crystals to amplify their metaphysical properties.

★ Shells: Although shells are not technically a crystal, but rather a natural elemental material, they are associated with love and are sacred to Aphrodite, the Greek love goddess, and are often used in magic talismans to attract romance.

★ ESSENTIAL OILS ★

The following essential oils are known for their aphrodisiac or love-attracting properties also, and can be worn as perfumes on the skin, used in an oil burner or vaporiser, dispersed in a bath, used in spell-casting and wishing rituals, sprinkled on your pillow to imbue your dreams with inspired romantic notions, or in any other creative ways you can think of! **

★ Essential oils, flowers and herbs which contain natural pheromones or like substances, or increase pheromone levels in the body, are: Lavender, Frankincense, Jasmine, Nutmeg, Ylang, Sandalwood, Patchouli and Asian Agarwood (Oud).

★ The prime love oil, which holds Universal appeal, is rose. Reputedly excellent for both the mind and body, roses are the basis of more than 95 per cent of women's fragrances, and the petals have a long tradition of uplifting the spirits and soothing the soul. *Rosa damascena* is believed to be good for attracting love, while R. *centifolia*, the French rose oil base, is regarded as an aphrodisiac. Rose is traditionally accepted as the all-encompassing Universal fragrance of love, blessed with a reputation for opening up the hearts of all those who come under its spell.

★ Cedarwood oil has been used since ancient times in incense and perfumes. Its deep, woody scent helps to stimulate the Base chakra, increasing sexual passion and desire. Its sedative qualities aid relaxation and encourage openness. In herbal magic, it is also associated with spells for wealth and abundance.

★ Neroli, Geranium, Almond (as a base), Basil, Thyme, Vetiver, Gardenia, Vanilla, Rose Otto, Apple, Cardamom, Lotus, Orange, Ginger, Bergamot, Rosewood and Clary Sage are also exquisitely seductive and sensual, and can be used in any way you like to bring to you that which your heart desires. These oils, when mixed with your own pheromones and magical intentions, will naturally enhance your point of attraction!

** Always research first and use with caution.

TAURUS ★ LOVE STYLE

"There's nothing small about Taurus, including her capacity for lasting love."
Linda Goodman

Taurus, ruled by the planet of love Venus, is in love with love. You need security, affection and stability like no other sign. Because you're so very conscious of stability, it is a rare Taurean who has many fleeting love affairs. You are strongly attracted to the opposite sex, but will never engage in aggressive pursuit of anybody; you would prefer to passively attract others to you. Seductive and sensuous but faithful and reliable, you are a good-natured, caring lover with a strong sense of family and the need for quiet and peace in your life. The Taurus female particularly can unequivocally be called a lady. She has a strong feminine vibration, good taste and a pronounced feeling for harmony and comfort.

Discreet charm is a strong feature of Tauruses of both genders, and although you are rarely adverse to flirtation, you will not give away your heart and soul until you know that your potential partner is genuine and in it for the long haul. An enduring and loyal partner, you never wish to be involved in a detached or open relational situation as this does not suit your style. Easy going but steadfast, if your partner makes you feel insecure or demands too much freedom, you may ask them to walk out *your* door; however, you are unlikely to attract this type of partnership in the first place. Your feelings are strong, deep, sincere and often silent, and you do not conquer by storm or force, but romantically, tenderly and sentimentally. Ruled by your senses, and especially touch, cuddling, affection and physical closeness are very important to you, and an undemonstrative partner will leave you cold. Protection and economic security is also vital to your wellbeing in any partnership, so you often unconsciously seek out a partner who can provide for and protect you, or a partner who you yourself can provide for and protect - the nurturing instinct comes naturally to you and being a homemaker is compatible with your nature. Although stubborn and sometimes too rooted in the one spot, your dependability and big-heartedness in relationships is second to none.

LUCKY IN LOVE?
TAURUS COMPATIBILITY

* Please note the following is based on your Sun sign alone. For a whole and integrated approach to relationship compatibility, your whole natal chart would need to be taken into consideration. Synastry (*syn*: acting or considered together, united; *astry*: pertaining to the stars) is a branch of astrology which delves into more complex areas, and is based upon the natal charts of the two people concerned, to determine overall compatibility, potential conflicts and suitability based upon celestial influences. For the purposes of length, the below information is simplified and only refers to Sun sign connections.

Taurus ★ Aries ♉ ♈

With Taurus's cautious Earthy ways, she finds Aries' impatience and haste difficult to handle. Yet the Ram will nonetheless intrigue and interest the Bull. Calm and steady Taurus soothes Aries's fiery haste, but the agile and quick-minded Ram might find the Bull a bit staid, unadventurous, unmoving, boring, slow and fixed. Fire with Earth is not an easy combination and since your needs, natures and tastes are so very different, there may be difficulties unless a compromise is reached - and neither of you are good at compromising. Aries thrives on the stimulus of new enterprises or challenges, whereas Taurus prefers peace, stability and reading the stock market reviews over a mug of hot chocolate or aged whisky. Very different in character, you have little in common. Taurus is possessive and 'stuck', while Aries values independence, adventure and movement; Taurus is simple, sensual and seeks security, while Aries is bold, experimental and seeks novel experiences; Taurus deals with tangible and practical realities while Aries is idealistic and can't cope with the mundane details of everyday life. There is potential for the frequent locking of horns that may hinder this relationship's progress - both of you are strong-willed, but in completely different ways. Taurus finds it difficult to understand Aries's dynamic and careless nature, while the Bull's need for tranquillity, domesticity, comfort, reliability and security could drag the Ram's unstoppable character down. As well, Aries becomes irritated and impatient by the Taurean's unhurried, stay-put and obstinate attitudes, and sensible Taurus will not tolerate Aries's extravagance and carelessness with her most precious resource - money. However, the Bull could help stabilise the restless Arien spirit and the Ram could assist the Taurean to lighten up and be a bit more spontaneous. If you can learn these lessons from each other without resentment brewing, you may have a slight chance of making it work. Just expect a lot of brooding and sulky behaviour if your relationship encounters a rocky period.

Overall compatibility rating ★ 6 out of 10

Lucky Romance Tip ★ To attract an Aries, wear the colours red or orange, and use the crystal diamond

Taurus ★ Taurus ♉ ♉

When you two Bulls get together, it's indulgence and then some! Be careful not to get too stuck in a rut - variety and a change from routine is important in this relationship to stop it becoming rigid or stale. On the whole though, you get along well with each other. Earth and Earth produces a very stable, conservative, down-to-Earth association and your relationship has strong enduring qualities because you both have a desire to maintain the status quo at all costs. You are at risk of following a lifestyle which may become stodgy and staid, so occasionally doing something out of routine will re-ignite the spark. When provoked, you can both be possessive and jealous - and as stubborn as mules, neither of you backing down. This can lead to a locking of horns which will only mean your hooves get so stuck in the mud that your relationship boat will eventually sink into the quicksand; stalemates are a common occurrence in this combination. Also, because you both have a cautious, introverted, security-seeking outlook, your partnership can lack dynamic initiative, novelty and fresh, exciting adventure. You must also keep in mind that familiarity breeds contempt and beware not to allow comfort and convenience to mean you take each other for granted and stick together because you are too afraid of change. The devil you know is *not* always better. Taureans are generally conservative, preferring fact to fantasy. You are both doers, not dreamers, and you will regard whatever you do from a practical and realistic point of view. You make a great 'planning' team and can achieve some amazing goals together, as well as being persistent and determined to reach them. You may both be fixed and materialistic, which can cause the odd issue, but overall you are kind, affectionate and content, which makes for an effective - and long-lasting - team. Sensual and indulgent, you will also enjoy sharing good wine and food beside a warming fire - just don't expect long deep and meaningful conversations and you will both feel fulfilled.

Overall compatibility rating ★ 7.5 out of 10
Lucky Romance Tip ★ To attract another Taurus, wear the colours pink or green, and use the crystal rose quartz

Taurus ★ Gemini ♉♊

The talkative Twins may make the Bull's head spin. It's often one step forward, two steps back, as the Bull closes in and Gemini wriggles free. Taurus is the earthiest sign of all, while Airy Gemini is extremely restless, changeable and fickle - traits which are completely foreign to the immovable Bull. The Twins' love of constant change and variety can be unnerving for Taurus, who likes to stay put and works best in the confines of a consistent routine. Taureans take commitment very seriously, therefore Gemini needs to control his flirtatious behaviour. If you can both overcome your considerable differences, this is potentially a very happy pairing. The earthbound Bull can indeed complement Gemini's flighty fast-paced haste. Even though the Twins find it difficult to tolerate the Bull's possessiveness, the Taurean slow and smooth sensuality may fascinate and intrigue Gemini. The Gemini's Mutable, flexible nature may prove too difficult to handle for the Bull's fixed, steady, consistent nature, and the Gemini fickleness may upset the normally peaceful Taurus's harmony. Gemini may resent being 'possessed' by the security-seeking Bull, and will at all opportunities break free from any restrictions placed upon him - sometimes forever. The Twins are quick-witted and lightning fast with their thoughts, while Taurus likes to mull things over before reaching a very well-considered conclusion; as well, Gemini loves to share, exchange and talk, while Taurus prefers peace, harmony and to keep her ideas to her quiet self. Further, Taurus does not like to analyse or over-think, preferring to live for the sensations of the moment, and this may frustrate the intellectual, ever-thinking Gemini, whose mind sparks in all directions simultaneously. In this partnership, there will be little mental rapport, and although Gemini may be initially attracted to Taurus's deep sensuality and grace of movement, his mind changes like the wind and he may well be off to seek greener pastures as soon as the Bull utters the words 'exclusive relationship'. The Taurus will ultimately perceive the Twins as too spirited and over-the-top, but if she can overcome her over-emphasis on stability, the Gemini can bring the gifts of exuberance, youthful vigour and excitement into their ordinary everyday life, and snuff out any stale boredom for good.

Overall compatibility rating ★ 6 out of 10

Lucky Romance Tip ★ To attract a Gemini, wear the colours light blue or yellow, and use the crystal citrine

Taurus ★ Cancer ♉ ♋

With your Earthy love of home and Cancer's Watery love of home, you two can definitely tango, but are both inclined to be clingy and possessive in your own different ways. Just bear in mind that Earth and Water can also create mud! But generally speaking, there is a natural affinity between your elements, so you will have more in common than not. The Cancerian will no doubt make the Taurean heart beat a little faster, in the most tender way possible. You both love comfort, security, warmth and protection, and your solid base is a very pronounced sense of family and home life. Feelings, emotions and affections are of paramount importance to both of you, and Taurus appreciates the attention, nurturing, sustenance and care which Cancer so enjoys giving. Taurus, who lives her life according to her senses, is a born epicure, and this will be compatible with the Cancerian's love of food - somehow the Bull instinctively knows that the way to Cancer's heart is through the stomach. Being basically conservative, cautious and conventional, conflicts and clashes are unlikely, however the Crab's strong emotions and moods could make the normally unshakable Bull feel a little unsettled at times. This should be a fairly easy and effortless union, for both of you can create a very comfortable and sharing environment, and although different in many ways, your differences are complementary rather than divisive, so you make each other feel safe and supported. The Bull will just need to be ultra-sensitive to avoid crushing the Crab's shell.

Overall compatibility rating ★ 8.5 out of 10
Lucky Romance Tip ★ To attract a Cancerian, wear the colours silver or white, and use the crystal moonstone

Taurus ★ Leo ♉ ♌

The sleepy Bull challenges the Lion's need for drama and excitement, and Leo may find it difficult when Taurus tries to possess him or shows little enthusiasm for his grandiose plans or ideals. Although both Fixed types, you express this quality in different ways. If Taurus enjoys and praises Leo's posturing while gently holding her own ground, she might find a whole new world. You are both extravagant, with a love of luxury, good quality things, and material pleasures, which is a mutual and advantageous aspect to your relationship. But Earth with Fire in two such strong-willed signs can cause conflict and opposition unless you both learn to compromise and practice some give and take. Leo thrives on the attention, affection and adoration which Taurus so readily and naturally gives to her special loved one, while Taurus appreciates Leo's fine taste, chivalry, big heart, demonstrative nature and unrivalled sense of style. Usually the Bull is quite content to be dominated by her Lion, but if she tolerates it for too long without saying anything, she can charge like her namesake!

Leo's big, often grandiose ideas can be unsettling for the conservative Taurus, and Taurus's inflexibility and dull nature may grate on the buoyant, dynamic Leo's nerves. If you can capitalise on your mutual love of indulgent pleasures such as good food, wine, art, leisure and theatre, this relationship stands a good, solid chance of surviving - after all, the Fixed signs are known for their endurance and stoic perseverance, and this could prove a fine example.

Overall compatibility rating ★ 7 out of 10
Lucky Romance Tip ★ To attract a Leo, wear the colours gold or orange, and use the crystal ruby

Taurus ★ Virgo ♉ ♍

Taurus and Virgo, both being of the Earth element, will enjoy an exquisitely sensual relationship, but you also risk falling into a stifling, dull routine. Virgo enjoys the Bull's Earthy generosity and affection, but resent their stubbornness. Two Earth signs like you speak the same language and have the same sensual approach to love. Remember though that Virgo prefers quality to quantity! Although you are not the most adventurous of pairings, you get on considerably well since you share a need for steadiness, consistency and dependability. You are both practical by nature and prefer routine, but this may lead to a rather mundane existence where one or both of you become stuck in a rut and feel unable to move. Taurus, who is deeply affectionate and in need of physical rapport, may find the Virgo a bit distant and undemonstrative. The Virgin is also aloof and analytical, two traits the Bull doesn't possess, and these could leave Taurus cold. Taurus also likes to possess and feel needed and loved and can therefore smother Virgo, whose feelings are tightly under control. Virgo gives a veiled love, while Taurus exudes a warm, flowing style of love, so you could clash in this area. You are both realistic however, and can usually resolve any issues around intimacy with good old-fashioned problem-solving skills - for both of you are pragmatic, capable and thorough, and you apply these skills to any adverse relationship situations you may encounter. Virgo's intellectuality and emphasis on the mental side of life could also be alien to the more physically-oriented Bull, who couldn't give a hoof about analysing anything. Virgo's fussiness, cleanliness and obsessiveness may unnerve Taurus, who just likes simple comforts and pleasures. Overall though, this is a very promising, albeit sensible, relationship. The bond of your common interests should ensure a strong relationship, which is characterised by faithfulness, reliability and steadfastness.

Overall compatibility rating ★ 8.5 out of 10
Lucky Romance Tip ★ To attract a Virgo, wear the colours white or yellow, and use the crystal sapphire

Taurus ★ Libra ♉ ♎

Mutually ruled by the lovely Venus, you both represent different aspects of this planet. The slow Taurean may seem conservative and too strait-laced for the Libran's ethereally romantic spirit. Since you are both ruled by the famed planet of love, you should have a lot in common - however, Earth and Air don't blend easily, and Libra is guided by the intellect while Taurus is led by its senses. But Taurus will be no doubt be intrigued and captivated by the graceful, easy going and charming Scales, and his chivalrous nature will win the Bull's heart. Both of you are warm, affectionate, sensuous and aesthetically aware by nature, and share a love of the arts, beauty and luxurious things. Taurus could be a little materialistic for the more ethereal and idealistic Libra, and being an Air sign, Libra will not tolerate being possessed by the clingy Bull. Security is the last thing on the Scales' mind, as they would prefer to share a deep mental affinity in their relationships, and see love as one of the many pleasures in life to be enjoyed without great attachment. Taurus will also not appreciate the naturally flirty Libra's wandering eye either, and will become jealous and brooding if she suspects Libra of being unfaithful. Being a Cardinal Air sign, the Scales will resent any restrictions to their freedom of movement, especially in social circles, in which they thrive. The Bull would rather dwell in the comfort of her home while Libra would much prefer to be on the social circuit; this major difference between you could give rise to substantial conflict. Overall, your mutual ruling planet Venus may well provide the bond that can glue you together, and because harmony and peace are vitally important to both of you, neither one is likely to provoke discord in the relationship. Although Taurus is stubborn, Libra can tactfully and cleverly manipulate the Bull's obstinacy into submission without the Bull even knowing it. Also, Libra is the sign of marriage and partnership, so this could link in well with Taurus's urge for relational security - or if your love breaks down, you could still make fine business partners, as you both have an innate sense for business and enterprise.

Overall compatibility rating ★ 7.5 out of 10
Lucky Romance Tip ★ To attract a Libran, wear the colours pink and blue, and use the crystal opal

Taurus ★ Scorpio ♉ ♏

Being Scorpio's natural opposite, the Bull holds a deep appeal to the Scorpion. Their common sense and physical sensuality turning the Scorpion on, but their stubbornness and lack of passion may equally put the Scorpio off. But generally, opposites attract and Earthy types like Taurus generally appreciate the sensitivity of a Water sign. Just be careful that your mutual passion doesn't turn into a locking-of-the-horns/claws competition. Although Earth is usually compatible with Water, your opposition status could prove difficult. Taurus and Scorpio are drawn to each other and an initially physical attraction may bring you together, but when this initial lust settles down a bit, the pendulum may swing the other way unless you have other strong things in common. Both highly sexed and incredibly sensual, there will inevitably be erotic overtones and emotional power plays. But even though you are compatible and even explosive in the bedroom, Scorpio's intensity and depth may unnerve the much simpler and uncomplicated Taurus. Mutual trust is absolutely essential, as Scorpio is prone to be suspicious and Taurus is prone to be jealous - you are both possessive, and (the wrong type of) sparks could fly if one of you catches the other even looking in someone else's direction. It is important to keep in mind that a raging Bull charges, and an enraged Scorpion stings; and neither experience is pleasant. Such intense feelings can also create a love-hate relationship, and emotions and resentfulness may run deep. The greatest potential threats to your relationship are your making of possessive demands on each other, and your jealousy. Trust may also be an issue; if the Scorpion doesn't trust the Bull, Taurus will be deeply crushed. Therefore, tolerance and understanding of each other's differing - but also complementary - natures must be exercised for this relationship to work successfully.

Overall compatibility rating ★ 7 out of 10
Lucky Romance Tip ★ To attract a Scorpio, wear the colours red or burgundy, and use the crystal malachite

Taurus ★ Sagittarius ♉ ♐

Totally different from the Archer in almost every regard, to the Sagittarius the Bull is either an interesting enigma or just 'too hard'. For the Archer's flighty spirit, Taurus might just be too cautious, slow, materialistic and dogmatic. Sagittarian Fire can make Taurus feel like the parched Earth, with all his ideas and plans. Yet the Archer makes the Bull giggle and teaches her to lighten up. However, even though the

Archer may impart some great lessons to the Bull and vice versa, you are very different by nature. Taurus is one of the most stable, consistent, down-to-Earth signs who only feels safe and secure when life is settled and predictable. Taurus's strong desire to put down roots and possess her loved one, sometimes to the point of smothering them with affection, is at great odds with the Sagittarian need to feel free, independent and able to explore and wander at whim. Sagittarius is a Fire sign, enjoys change, seeks distant horizons and needs plenty of room to move around both mentally and physically. This will threaten the Bull's strong need for comfort, security and sameness. Taurus dwells on the material plane, while the Archer resides in the philosophical, intangible realms - another divisional point of difference between you two. While Sagittarius is broad-visioned and open-minded, Taurus lives in the physical senses and her perception on most areas of life will invariably begin and end with these. But the Taurean sensuality will intrigue and attract the amorous Sagittarius, and both of you have charm by the bucket-loads with which to win each other over. You are both loving of luxury and extravagance, but Taurus is more restrictive and practical, which could frustrate the far more liberal and fancy-free Archer, who spends money carelessly. Overall, temperaments are likely to clash in this pairing, but if the Bull can keep a tighter rein on her need to possess and the Archer can be content to cuddle up on the couch from time to time, this relationship could very well work.

Overall compatibility rating ★ 7 out of 10
Lucky Romance Tip ★ To attract a Sagittarius, wear the colour deep purple or royal blue, and use the crystal zircon

Taurus ★ Capricorn ♉ ♑

Two Earth signs combine to create stability, security and shared aspirations. The Goat feels right at home with the Bull, yet together you may get bogged down in routine, stuck in a rut and the shine may quickly disappear from your romance. But overall, the lusty Bull and the horny Goat make a pleasing combination. With Capricorn's strength and Taurus's good taste, you could build an empire together - or never leave home! Taurus admires Capricorn's ambition, goal-mindedness and will for advancement, and the Capricorn appreciates the Bull's nurturing, sensuous, solid nature. You two seem to have a natural affinity and agreement that promises lasting happiness. The Bull may even help the Goat to loosen up a little and relax her self-control. Security-conscious Taurus will resonate with Capricorn's practical, basic attitudes, realistic approach, perseverance and conservatism. Being Earth signs, you are both likely to be sensible, reasonable, patient and responsible, so most issues can be worked through in a rational, logical manner. Big, burning flames of passion may be absent here, and there is a danger that life could become a little too serious at times, but injecting some light-hearted fun and frivolous activities into your time together, should ease this very easy-to-solve problem. Indeed, you have great potential to grow old together.

Overall compatibility rating ★ 9 out of 10
Lucky Romance Tip ★ To attract a Capricorn, wear the colours brown or black, and use the crystal garnet

Taurus ★ Aquarius ♉ ♒

Aquarians can make you see red - with either passion or anger! Either way, they easily slip out of your grasp and fly off into the world of ideas and freedom - and at the most unexpected times! Very different in nature, you have little in common except your more negative expressions, such as stubbornness, unwillingness to change and inflexibility. Taurus is possessive while Aquarius values freedom; Taurus is affectionate while Aquarius is generally cool; Taurus is simple while Aquarius embraces complexities; Taurus is sensual and seeks security while Aquarius is experimental and seeks novel experiences; Taurus is traditional while Aquarius challenges the establishment; Taurus is domestic while Aquarius loathes being chained to the kitchen sink; Taurus deals with tangible and practical realities while Aquarius is idealistic and dwells in the abstract and unusual. Both share the Fixed mode, meaning there is a certain obstinacy and potential for frequent locking of horns that may hinder their progress. Taurus finds it difficult to understand Aquarius's unconventional and unpredictable nature, while Aquarians spread themselves far and wide socially, finding it difficult to fulfil Taurus's need for exclusivity in a relationship.

Overall compatibility rating ★ 5 out of 10
Lucky Romance Tip ★ To attract an Aquarian, wear the colours electric blue or turquoise, and use the crystal aquamarine

Taurus ★ Pisces ♉ ♓

Tender Pisces melts Taurus's heart and waters her seeds of desire. But if the earthbound Bull tries to crush Pisces's dreams, the slippery Fish will swim away. Although Pisces is extremely flexible and adaptable, and Taurus essentially inflexible and unchanging, you do share similar natures, being peaceful, placid, kind and gentle. This combination of Earth and Water is very compatible because your ruling planets, Neptune and Venus, also share similar qualities, Neptune being the higher octave of Venus, vibrating at a higher frequency but still exerting a complementary influence. While Taurus is possessive and Pisces is 'slippery', these two can make their relationship work if they capitalise on their romantic and affectionate natures. Challenges may arise if the Taurean tendency towards materialism is not controlled, as Pisces never seeks to own or possess, only to understand; one thing the Fish cannot understand, however, is the Bull's need for luxury, ownership and 'having' things. Both are sensual, easy going, friendly, artistic, soft, romantic, have a love of beauty and appreciate life's pleasures. These two seem to have just as many differences as similarities, and as a result, have the potential to ultimately balance each other out. Taurus is down-to-Earth while Pisces floats up in the clouds; the realist complements the dreamer; Taurus deals with tangible and practical realities while Pisces is inherently impractical and other-worldly. If the Bull keeps her feet firmly planted in the ground and maintains patience with the wanderings of the oft elusive Fish, she will find that the Fish will always swim back when she's ready - or at least return to Earth to pick the Bull up on her magical carpet so that the Taurean spirit can soar amongst the clouds as well. If Pisces can understand and fulfil Taurus's need for exclusivity in a relationship, and withstand the Bull's tight grip, these two have much potential - if a little clouded over by emotion at times.

Overall compatibility rating ★ 6.5 out of 10
Lucky Romance Tip ★ To attract a Pisces, wear the colours mauve or sea green, and use the crystal amethyst

YOUR TAROT CARDS ★ FOR LUCK, MAGIC, ENERGY, ABUNDANCE, QUESTING & MEANING
THE HIEROPHANT, THE EMPRESS & THE WORLD

Tarot and astrology are inextricably linked. All the cards of the Major Arcana, which comprises 22 of the Tarot's 78 cards, are 'ruled by' or connected with either one of the twelve zodiac signs, the planets and luminaries, or one of the four elements.

The 22 Major Arcana cards contain the richest symbolism of all the cards in the Tarot deck, each carrying a myriad of messages for the reader to decipher. The symbolism contained within these images represents the archetypal aspects of your character. It also describes the path your soul takes through each stage of life, revealing clues through which you can explore different parts of yourself. Each of the cards also represents an aspect of Universal human experience and has a name that either directly conveys the meaning of the card, such as Strength or Justice, or depicts individuals that represent these human archetypes, such as the Hermit or the Empress. The illustrations on each card contain one or more figures and tuning into a card's imagery enables you to grasp its meaning intuitively. Consider the demeanour of the characters, whether it is day or night, the background, any symbols, the buildings, the colours, the vegetation, the weather and the season. Every card has its own story to impart, and through entering that story you can gain deeper insights into the full picture of your journey so far, as well as illuminating your path ahead.

I have outlined three cards here for your sign: The Hierophant, The Empress and The World, all of which have links to your zodiac sign itself Taurus, your ruling planet Venus, and your element of Earth. All three cards will have special meaning for your sign, and can carry powerful messages and lessons for you to reflect upon.

★ THE HIEROPHANT ★
Ruled by Taurus

Keywords ★ Advice, Wisdom, Enlightenment

★ KEY THEMES ★
Search for Meaning in Life ★ Longing for Spiritual Enlightenment ★ Mentors and Guides ★ Traditional Viewpoints or Methods ★ Schools, Spiritual Institutions and Organisations ★ Spiritual Wisdom and Development ★ Questing ★ Learning ★ Benevolence ★ Stability ★ Rigidity ★ An Experienced, Older Man ★ Sense of Right and Wrong

Number ★ 5
Astrological Sign ★ Taurus

THE MESSAGE ★ Society's larger traditional values are represented by the Hierophant, sometimes called the Pope. Jungian theorists assign the archetype of the persona to this card, the social mask we all wear when we are out in the world. This concept is also associated with your astrological Ascendant, or the mask you wear in public. The Hierophant indicates there is a search for meaning underway in your life. Seek out mentors, experts and like-minded friends. The Hierophant is a conservative, patient man who appreciates stability and tradition. He is quietly persevering, and offers a chance to examine spirituality as a means for understanding life's changes.

THE STORY ★ The Hierophant represents spiritual wisdom and is the mediator between heaven and Earth. He is a great teacher, always compassionate and fair. A sympathetic ruler, he listens and is merciful. He has breadth of vision and is able to encompass and understand all facets of human needs. He emphasises the importance of learning and the role of the individual in society. He is depicted in the Tarot as an old man - wise, placid, patient and merciful - whose guidance is practical but follows, without question, the dogma as taught by his predecessors. His goals are the maintaining of social mores, and the assured position of his religion or spiritual leaning. This 'father confessor' can be relied on for advice and support, within the guidelines of his training. And while he faithfully lays down the codified laws and principles contained in his book, his unremitting daily study and practice of those traditions still impart to him some of the occult knowledge upon which his religion was originally based.

THE LESSON ★ The Hierophant is the male counterpart of the High Priestess. But whereas she is concerned with intuitive wisdom, the Hierophant is more connected with the concept of moral law. We consult the Hierophant about the great questions of the soul which sometimes torture the mind; we ask for his benediction. The Hierophant can be regarded as the spiritual master representing the higher powers and forces, who through his role and his presence, reminds us that we are mortal, fallible, and that we must put our trust in him as much as in ourselves. The Hierophant has three stages of grace - faith, hope and charity - of which he is a symbol. He is a man to whom you can confide, and a good advisor, who will offer enlightened support, help and backing. But the Hierophant insists that if you seek his guidance, that you follow his example and adhere to the rules, thereby setting a good example for others. He also encourages you to walk the path that you choose for yourself, because he knows that learning through experience - after being taught by example - is the best way.

SYMBOLISM *★ In simple terms, the Hierophant represents a teacher. He represents the teaching of, and adherence to, a set of beliefs that act as a spiritual guide in life. In most Tarot decks this card is titled 'The Pope', connecting it to the Christian faith. In other decks, it is called The Hierophant, which implies any form of esoteric teaching that holds a personal value or meaning for you. This card ultimately symbolises the advice given from a perpetrator of wisdom of understanding, and your role is to respect this advice, but also to listen to your inner core of wisdom and access the knowledge you already hold which enables you to govern your own life. Therefore, this card also symbolises your higher self.

In most decks the Hierophant is seated on a throne between two pillars, raising his hand to bless his priests. At his feet are two crossed keys, both made out of gold (sometimes gold and silver), which symbolise the expression of both insight and logic. The triple cross and three-tiered crown featured in the card represent the Divine, intellectual and physical worlds. In Christian terms, bearing in mind this card is often titled 'the High Priest' or 'The Pope', they relate to the trinity of Father, Son and Holy Spirit.

In some decks there is a bird at the Hierophant's feet, symbolising the spirit, flapping its wings, denoting the god's rulership over spiritual *and* temporal matters.

The Hierophant, or High Priest, is a man of great knowledge, a medicine man, the one who finds and prescribes a remedy, a mediator. This word also derives from medium; the intermediary, the messenger. And this is very much the role played by the Hierophant, high priest of knowledge, whose wisdom relieves, liberates and fortifies our minds, bodies and souls.

At its best the Hierophant is a benevolent teacher, kind and understanding. This card symbolises a wise and capable advisor, forgiveness and comfort, the influence of established faith and the power of the conscious mind. He represents a teacher and rules to get along by, being concerned with the concept of moral laws. Its divinatory meanings are ritualism, kindness, mercy, inspiration, forgiveness, compassion, servitude, timidity, overt reserve, captivity to one's own ideas, conformity, a religious or spiritual leader, and sometimes a tendency to cling to ideas and principles, long after they have become outdated.

The Hierophant essentially stands for spiritual enlightenment. As a priest or holy man, he represents those who wish to expand their understanding of the meaning of life. Unlike the Emperor whose interests lie primarily in material matters, the Hierophant's interests are planted firmly in spirituality. He is attracted by the search for truth, philosophical and spiritual, and is not bound by any particular religion or dogma (despite the Christian connotations in some interpretations and imagery).

The Hierophant often represents an older man who has knowledge and wisdom and great experience of life. He is a man you could confide in, a sound advisor, and wise and enlightened supporter. He is a man from whom you could ask a recommendation, a right or an authorisation. He may be a judge, a barrister, a doctor or a knowledgeable, respected and cultured man in a high-powered position who is perhaps responsible for some important mission.

Taureans are recommended to carry one of these cards with them to illumine their paths, and to magnetise that for which they are asking. Go forth and claim the magic which is yours by using the symbolism of the Hierophant as your guide!

★ THE EMPRESS ★
Ruled by Venus

Keywords ★ Nurturance, Fertility, Security

★ KEY THEMES ★
Creation ★ Fertility ★ Emotional Wealth ★ Motherhood ★ Happy, Stable Relationships ★ Growth ★ Lavish Abundance ★ Birthing and Fostering Dreams ★ Art ★ Creativity ★ Affinity with Nature ★ Security ★ Pleasure ★ Harmony ★ Material Comforts ★ Fruitfulness ★ Ripeness ★ Mother ★ Wife

Number ★ 3
Astrological Signs ★ Taurus & Libra

THE MESSAGE ★ The Empress can be linked to the Full Moon, which, upon reaching its shining bright potential, must slowly fade into the darkness and become a mere sliver. This Earthly mother teaches about the wisdom of nature, its rhythms and cycles of growth, death and rebirth, and the idea that these cycles are present within all humans. She also imparts knowledge about women and their ways and needs, leading by example. The Empress, the archetypal fertile Earth Mother, can help bring daydreams to fruition in a world where logic and intuition should dwell together as heaven and Earth do. As such, the Empress is telling you to give birth to your dreams, to nurture yourself and others, spend time in nature, and indulge in creative and artistic endeavours. She suggests a possible pregnancy, a harmonious home environment and progress with your plans. She encourages you to enjoy material comforts and sexual fulfilment but to be wary of overindulgence. Enjoy the beautiful things in life, knowing that you deserve to be exquisitely and Divinely provided for.

THE STORY ★ The Empress represents the Great Mother, pure and simple. She promises abundance, birth, growth, harmony, community, and relationship. She can represent the Earth from which all life is born, and to which it returns at the end of its cycle. The first Empress-type statues were the small pregnant 'Venus' figurines from the Ice Age in Europe and Russia (at least 30,000 BC). These tiny goddess figures are pregnant to bursting point and generally without distinctive features of face, hands or feet - the emphasis clearly lay upon their full breasts and bellies. Much feminine wisdom has faded with the rise of patriarchal societies in our modern lives, but we still hold the basis for these mysteries within our bodies. The Empress in her contemporary 'seductress' pose symbolises the unconscious knowledge modern women share of the ancient mysteries and female reverence, of healing and transformation, that live on in our much-diminished but ever-pure Divinity. The Empress feels her connection to the Earth. She knows - has always known - the mystery of procreation, the potential for growing and nurturing life, the sacred act of birthing, and the communal life close to the soil - a time when people did not make war, but spent their leisure time making love and art. The Empress is a sensual, practical woman who appreciates good, wholesome, hearty food, nature and a simple life. She is nurturing and generous, and teaches that you need to foster dreams and desires. If the card preceding this, the High Priestess, holds the secrets of life, then the Empress is what gives that life soul and emotion, for she represents the understanding and the power of that life. The Empress's power lies primarily in feelings, as she is able to exploit both the riches of the heart and the psyche.

THE LESSON ★ This is a warmly emotional card, suggesting love, luxury and comfort. The Empress brings out your artistic side, opens your love of beauty, and heightens your aesthetic appreciation. The Empress represents 'prosperity thinking' and the power of positive imagination. The Empress is a materially and practically inclined card rather than psychically- or spiritually-oriented, although she does have links with the Divine feminine. Your hopes *will* come to fruition, finances *will* improve, green leaves *will* sprout, examples and symbols of fertility *will* abound, and you *will* begin to feel more confident as you reap the rewards of your efforts. And indeed, ask the Great Mother for what you need. Remember, Venus (Ishtar-Aphrodite) is the wishing star.

SYMBOLISM * ★ The Empress is the third numbered card in the Major Arcana. The number three is indicative of synthesis and harmony, childbirth and maternal productivity. The Empress is shown as an Earth Mother, gentle and caring, surrounded by comfort and plenitude. Her crown is surmounted by twelve stars representing the signs of the zodiac. The Empress, as the Earth Mother, sometimes appears in a field of corn, symbolising her link with nature. She has a strong connection with motherhood and is portrayed as pregnant, or at least wearing a flowing outfit which hints at it. She has been called 'the star-crowned empress, herself the morning star'. This is a direct identification with the goddess Venus, otherwise known as 'the morning star', who, as well as her famed associations with love, is also a deity connected with fruitfulness and harvest.

Still other cards depict a beautiful, serene woman with long, flowing fair hair that resembles the golden fields of corn, dotted with poppies, surrounding her. A waterfall and forest can be seen beyond the rich fields, and at her feet a horn of plenty overflows with fruit, symbolising the Earth's abundant bounty. The Empress is a symbol of potential possibly fulfilled by the hint of pregnancy that her loose and flowing robe suggests. Her robe is adorned with seeded-pomegranates, her lap contains a sheaf of corn, and she wears a necklace of ten pearls, symbolising the ten planets that comprise the Solar system. The twelve stars in her crown represent the twelve months of the year, the twelve signs of the zodiac, and the twelve hours each of day and night; she wears a necklace with four stones, standing for the four seasons of life: birth, blossom, fruition and decay; indeed, all these life stages and processes are presided over by the Empress, and this imagery points to natural cycles, growth, abundance, fertility, and the ever-present possibilities of new life.

The left hand of the Empress points towards the sky and the heavens. Her right hand holds a spectre pointing to the ground, symbolising her anchorage to the Earth. She also holds a protective shield with the symbol of an eagle, and is normally depicted in natural surroundings with a stream flowing behind her. The position of her hands connects her with the Magician card and shows that she is the primal creative force, representing motherhood and security, in a way that ultimately brings together heaven and Earth.

The Empress nurtures and nourishes, representing any process that involves physical growth and sustenance. She represents a time of passion, a period during which we approach life through feelings and pleasure rather than thought and ideas. This passion can be either sexual or motherly; either way, it is deeply experienced. Marriage, children, and issues involving motherhood and creativity will be positively affected when this card shows up.

The Empress reveals that it is time for birth, whether literal or creative. Whatever has been gestating in the previous card, The High Priestess, is now ready to be born. When she appears in a spread, she denotes a time of growth, of flourishing crops, creative ideas and all things reaching their full maturity.

Ultimately, the Empress represents happy, stable relationships, growth and fertility. This card is a symbol of fulfilled potential, creative pursuits, the satisfaction of nurturing something to fruition (as well as the pain of its loss), and symbolises love, marriage and motherhood. Its divinatory meanings are feminine progress, fruitfulness, pregnancy, security, mother, sister, wife, marriage, children, feminine influence, practicality, accomplishment, nurturing, and the ability to gently motivate others.

★ THE WORLD/UNIVERSE ★
Ruled by Saturn & the Element of Earth

Keywords ★ Completion, Attainment, Fulfilment

★ KEY THEMES ★
★ Arrival! ★ Completion ★ Fulfilment of Hopes and Dreams ★ Crowning Achievement ★ Total Success ★ Dreams Come True ★ Expansion ★ Aspirations ★ Idealism ★ A Prize or Goal Reached ★ Acclaim ★ Graduation ★ Accomplishment ★ Attainment ★ Contentment ★ Gratitude ★ The Path Toward Enlightenment ★ Perfection ★ Freedom ★ A Move to the Next Level ★ Cosmic Awareness ★ Expanded Consciousness ★ Joy ★ Great Outlook ★

Meditation ★
"I have completed one journey and will now rebirth myself to begin a brand new one. I welcome every chance to grow and learn."

Number ★ 21

Astrological Signs ★ Capricorn, Taurus, Virgo & Aquarius

THE MESSAGE ★ You have arrived at the beginning of the Path to Enlightenment, or could be considerably advanced along it by now. The World card suggests a job well done - you have happily completed something of great significance. Enjoy these feelings of wholeness and completion as your amazing accomplishments have been well-earned. You're now ready to move onto something new. You have grown spiritually and have evolved to a whole new level in your understanding of the Universe and your place in it. As well as this, you have attained complete clarity, cosmic awareness, significant enlightenment, an expanded consciousness and above all, the true freedom that accompanies all this.

THE STORY ★ A statue of a woman has come to life and is dancing, looking back at a leaf she holds in her outstretched hand. Just as the Earth, Divine Mother of us all, evolved from the stars and materialised into reality, so have our physical selves been created out of the same essence so that we may dance the dance of life just as She dances through the cosmos. This dream-like journey is one of going deep within and finding our essential harmony with All There Is. When we arrive at the knowledge of who we really are we gain The World.

THE AWAKENING ★ The World is a symbol of accomplishment, of an end which is also a beginning. The journey is completed! Upon reaching the World your goal is attained and you are suffused with joy and fulfilment. Life is fully and rapturously embraced, and you are free to experience all that it offers. You realise that the end of a journey merely leads to the first step on a new one. By uniting and balancing your long-sought after inner harmony with the skills you have learned in this lifetime so far, you have achieved true success and The World can be yours. Although hard work has been required to attain this, material rewards and inner peace are promised. But overall, you must view your life in the context of the whole of life and All There Is, before you can gain the wisdom you seek. The World imparts the message that each one of us carries a world inside of us, which is neither unattainable, illusory or utopian. It is simply what we are. All the elements are gathered here so that our conscience may awaken and our future will unfold as it is meant to before us.

SYMBOLISM *★ The World card symbolises completion and renewal. It incorporates the wisdom gathered throughout the journey of the previous 21 cards. The World embodies the essence of success, arrival, fulfilment and happiness. It shows a willingness to embrace life fully and to welcome in the new.

The central figure in the World card, hermaphroditic in appearance, symbolises the integration of the masculine and feminine principles to form a complete, unified entity. The wreath is a symbol of triumph, success, rebirth and renewal, while the surrounding creatures embody different aspects of human nature.

One of the most ancient symbols of alchemy is that of Ouroboros, the dragon or serpent which lies in a circle with its tail in its mouth. This sleeping creature must be awoken for its potential to be realised, and its energies released, for us to begin -

and achieve - the process of self-transformation. The circle around the dragon, a symbol without end and without beginning, symbolises the fact that one's beginning can also be found in its end, and vice versa. And so the symbol for Ouroboros never loses its meaning, for its meaning is eternity and in a sense the journey is never really completed; each ending is followed by a new beginning. Even if we eventually arrive back at the place where we first began our journey, nothing will be the same; all is transformed.

The World (or Universe), the final card of the Major Arcana, is the supreme symbol of unity and wholeness. It commonly depicts a dancing figure holding the Magician's wand and encircled by a laurel wreath. The wand is symbolic of the magic of self-transformation, while the laurel is the plant of success, victory and high achievement. The circle represents the Ouroboros (a serpent or dragon eating its own tail), a symbol of eternity. In each corner are the four Fixed signs of the zodiac: Taurus the Bull, Leo the Lion, Scorpio the Eagle and Aquarius the Man, which correspond to the four seasons of spring, summer, autumn and winter respectively, the four evangelical qualities of Man: humanity, spirituality, courage and strength, and also the four elements, which the alchemists combined to create a perfect fifth - the 'quintessence', or fifth element. This fifth element is symbolised by the central figure in the card, a genderless hermaphrodite, an image of the reconciliation of opposites, and also of balance. The card's number is twenty-one, the number of completion (three times seven, the two most magically significant numbers). The wreath may also represent zero, the symbol of infinity, with which you started the journey; therefore, the end of one journey is marking the beginning of another.

Astrologically, the World seems to be the most strongly related to the Mid-heaven, which is the highest point in the sky at the moment of birth. The World's divinatory meanings are completion, perfection, the rewards of labour, inner satisfaction, the end result of all your efforts, success, synthesis, fulfilment, capability, eternal life, admiration from others, ultimate change, and triumph in all your undertakings. As a symbol of completion, attainment, success and self-knowledge, she suggests that you remind yourself of what you have already achieved, and know that others are aware of you, appreciate and truly admire your past efforts. She tells you that you are now entering an extremely rewarding phase of your life when you will enjoy the benefits of all your hard work.

The World marks the end of a period of time, or the completion of a task, which has its new beginnings as a seed within. It denotes a time of celebration and the wonderful feelings that accompany any occasion during which something is finished, or made whole. It represents a deeply satisfying sense of achievement and fulfilment, suggestive of a peak experience - and expanded horizons ahead. On another level, however, any accomplishment or completion may be followed afterwards by a feeling of emptiness or deflation, as the goal has been realised and the dream made a reality. At this point, the crowned dancing figure who celebrates reaching the finishing mark, suddenly morphs again to embody a foetal-like being, waiting to re-evolve and rebirth itself as the Fool in the never-ending circular journey; in this way, The World symbolises the ending of one cycle and the commencement of another, and indeed The World represents a course that has now come full circle, and suggests you can rest on your laurels for a time before moving onto this next phase, as you have rightly earned it. You now understand your place within that system, and are ready to begin a new phase from the beginning, but this time with an elevated, higher sense of acquired wisdom, spiritual truth and inner knowing.

* Please note that the images described are not found in all Tarot decks. The images in different decks can differ considerably.

THE TAROT'S SUIT OF PENTACLES ★ REPRESENTING THE EARTH ELEMENT

The Pentacle, or five-pointed star, that symbolises Earth in nature magic is often displayed as a central feature on the Suit of Pentacles cards. The Pentacles (known in some old decks as Coins or Discs) represent the Earth element - the energy that keeps us grounded, and the physical or material side of life. They represent the outer manifestation of our spiritual nature, and signify fertility and fecundity in all its forms - sensuality, sensual pleasures, sex and procreation, and the grounding and anchoring of creative energy. The Pentacles tell you about your relationship with the material world, resources, status, tangible assets, and also with your work. Being of the Earth realm, the Pentacles are also associated with prosperity, hard work, financial progress and practical concerns. They can represent the mastery of life's material aspects, or the ambition and striving directed towards achieving them. In essence, the Pentacles are connected with matters that are financial, economic, monetary, or concerning stability. They highlight your attitudes to wealth, work, possessions and success. Dealing with the practicalities of life, they reflect our thinking and actions around earthlier issues, and can inform us of areas where we seek greater stability in our lives. You experience the story of the Pentacles through your relationship with the tangible, physical aspects of yourself - through your attitudes towards your body, sensuality, success, work and worldly goods. A healthy approach towards all of these provides you with a sense of confidence that deepens your perspective on life. Focusing on this suit can help us become more grounded and can reconnect you to life and creativity through linking your Earthy nature to your spiritual essence. The Pentacles provide a solid framework that can be used as a springboard to attainment. Without the foundation of the Pentacles, the effectiveness of the other suits and their elemental correspondences (emotional Water, intellectual Air and enterprising Fire) would be hindered. In a deck of playing cards, the Pentacles correspond to the suit of Diamonds.

THE LUCKY 13 ★ TAUREAN TIPS FOR INCREASED MAGIC, LUCK & MAGNETISM

1 ★ Incorporate Taurean symbols into your daily life to remind yourself of your soul's mission.

2 ★ Use the crystal Diamond in any form in your daily life - wear it, meditate with it, hold it and carry it with you everywhere! Diamond is the precious stone of Taurus *and* Venus, and symbolises love and endurance. It also brings fortitude, clarity, enlightenment and spiritual evolution. As a Universal symbol of wealth, it might even attract the material riches that Taureans instinctively desire to manifest. Above all, it is a solidified tonic which helps to strengthen bonds of all kinds, and attract wonderful things to you.

3 ★ Wear or surround yourself with the colours blue, green and rose pink.

4 ★ Learn the way of the Scorpion, by learning greater depth of thought, spirituality, transformation and renewal. Scorpio has much to teach the Taurean spirit. Swim down to the depths of the soul … Experience death and renewal in some form on a daily basis … Delve into what makes others tick … Cultivate more passion and intensity … Be moved … Enjoy the sensual feasts and fruits of your journey with gusto … Plunge into your inner self and feel the wonder of its vastness … it's all within you!

5 ★ Use your lucky numbers 1 and 6, whenever you are needing an extra stroke of luck.

6 ★ Magnify and celebrate your deep sensuality, your giving nature, your riches, your patience, your steadfastness, your dedication, your loyalty, and your strong sense of self.

7 ★ Remind yourself of your quest constantly, that is by speaking, breathing and *truly living* your dreams and goals - give them form, something you are very capable of!

8 ★ Focus your energies on exploring your inner depths, and transforming yourself through your higher spirit. Connect with your deep love of beauty, comfort, art and luxury, and inborn creativity through any means possible.

9 ★ Use your innate powers of aesthetic awareness and visualisation to draw that which you desire towards you. Remember that you don't always need to see something before you can believe it. If you can develop simple faith in the positive outcome of events, you can easily use your largely untapped intuition to great creative effect.

10 ★ Tap into and utilise your ability to provide for others, through sharing your material things, emotions, spirit and soul. But to do that, you'll need to abandon your fears, ease yourself gently off the ground and float into the soft, fluffy atmosphere - a wishing balloon might help! Release your inhibitions and fly.

11 ★ View your practical, down-to-Earth nature as a strength and call forth the powers of your pragmatic, productive and loving self. Be who you *really* are, without reservation or apology, and the rest will fall into place.

12 ★ Become the 'Dependable Provider' for others - and yourself - that you were born to be!

13 ★ Once you have mastered a greater spiritual focus and have dived a little deeper than you may feel comfortable with, learn to share the resulting abundance, insights and knowledge with others so they too can walk the Higher Path!

HAVE YOU PACKED YOUR MAGICAL BAG FOR THE JOURNEY?

If you wish to increase and draw more luck, love and abundance into your life, a power pack is essential. For Taureans, I would recommend carrying or wearing the following items on you on your travels. Then just sit back and watch as magic pours into your experiences and realities, both inner and outer!

★ One of each of the following gemstones: Diamond, Emerald, Sapphire, Jade, Rose Quartz
★ Tarot cards The Hierophant & The Empress (and The World/Universe card too, if you wish)
★ A beaver in any form
★ Something made of silver
★ An owl symbol in any form
★ A postcard or image from a cool, dry place (representing your Melancholic disposition). Bon Voyage!
★ A postcard from the future to yourself, proclaiming, 'Wish You Were Here!'

A FINAL WORD ★ TAPPING INTO THE MAGIC OF TAURUS

There is something inherently magical about Taurus, the gentle Bull. Nothing is hurried about you. The cosmos has endowed you with the precious and enviable gifts of calmness, comforting strength, consistency, stability, loyalty and steadfast devotion. Whether you are fully cognisant of it or not, a magical reservoir of energy is available to you to tap into whenever it is needed. Blessed with exquisite tastes and an eye for beauty, indulgence and luxury, you have a soothing, classy, simple air of style about you that others adore.

Inside anyone who has a strong Taurus influence in their natal chart, is a person who takes the long-term view and proceeds slowly but surely with an indomitable and unshakeable inner confidence, because Taurus is only interested in the best of everything, and they always get it - and then possess it with a fierce but quiet determination. Strong-willed and interested in the material realm, Taureans can also be greedy and cranky underneath their warm and sensual façade, and you fear losing control of your emotions, your money or your loved ones more than anything else. If you do lose control, it can be so devastating and disturbing to your deeply placid core, that it may take you a while to regain your composure. But recover you do so well, because you are nothing if not extremely resilient and robust. Your symbol the Bull typifies the potential explosive inner nature of your sign - for it is an animal which is strong and mostly calm, but can be provoked into intense and powerful rages. Thankfully, your serene nature and charming grace win out over any undesirable states of being, and you are the quintessential tortoise who always wins the race through your enchanting personality.

Finally, to attune yourself to luck, harmony and success, Taureans should wear, eat, inhale, meditate upon, create, design, and dance with any or all of the suggested luck-enhancers for your Sun sign to receive the most beneficial astral vibrations these 'boosters' can offer you. Wearing, decorating and working with the amazing powers of all your lucky guides, animals, crystals, colours, woods, cards, herbs, foods, places, talismans, planetary influences, charms, numbers, and other magical tips contained within the words of this very book, will bring you greater abundance, love, magic, energy, happiness and personal power, and attract all manner of things to you like bees to sweet flowers. This, my Taurean friends, I promise you - and Aquarians *never* lie.

Good luck on the rest of your amazing life journey, and may LUCK always smile upon you!

Lani is also available for personal Astrology, Numerology, Aura * & Tarot reading consultations, via post, email, Skype and in-person.

Please email lalana76@bigpond.com
for more information.

In-person only

Facebook Page ★ Astrology Magic

Other Books in the **Lucky Astrology** Series

Lucky Astrology ★ Aries
Lucky Astrology ★ Gemini
Lucky Astrology ★ Cancer
Lucky Astrology ★ Leo
Lucky Astrology★ Virgo
Lucky Astrology ★ Libra
Lucky Astrology ★ Scorpio
Lucky Astrology ★ Sagittarius
Lucky Astrology ★ Capricorn
Lucky Astrology ★ Aquarius
Lucky Astrology ★ Pisces

Order your copies now, from White Light Publishing House, at www.whitelightpublishingau.com

www.ingramcontent.com/pod-product-compliance
Lightning Source LLC
Chambersburg PA
CBHW071156300426
44113CB00009B/1227